TEN YEARS

A NOMAD

ALSO BY MATTHEW KEPNES

How to Travel the World on $50 a Day

Matthew Kepnes

TEN YEARS

A NOMAD

A Traveler's Journey Home

ST. MARTIN'S PRESS
New York

First published in the United States by St. Martin's Press, an imprint of
St. Martin's Publishing Group

TEN YEARS A NOMAD. Copyright © 2019 by Matthew Kepnes. All rights reserved.
Printed in the United States of America. For information, address St. Martin's
Publishing Group, 120 Broadway, New York, NY 10271.

www.stmartins.com

Library of Congress Cataloging-in-Publication Data

Names: Kepnes, Matt, author.
Title: Ten years a nomad : a traveler's journey home / Matthew Kepnes.
Other titles: 10 years a nomad
Description: First Edition. | New York : St. Martin's Press, [2019]
Identifiers: LCCN 2019006596 | ISBN 9781250190512 (hardcover) | ISBN
  9781250190529 (ebook)
Subjects: LCSH: Kepnes, Matt—Travel. | Travel writers—United States—
  Biography. | Voyages around the world—Biography. | Tourism.
Classification: LCC G154.5.K46 A3 2019 | DDC 910.4092 [B]—dc23
LC record available at https://lccn.loc.gov/2019006596

Our books may be purchased in bulk for promotional, educational, or business use.
Please contact your local bookseller or the Macmillan Corporate and Premium Sales
Department at 1-800-221-7945, extension 5442, or by email at
MacmillanSpecialMarkets@macmillan.com.

First Edition: July 2019

10 9 8 7 6 5 4 3 2 1

TO THE FIVE STRANGERS

ON THAT BUS IN THAILAND.

THANKS FOR PUSHING ME

ON THIS JOURNEY.

EVERY DAY

IS A JOURNEY,

AND THE

JOURNEY ITSELF

IS HOME.

—MATSUO BASHŌ

CONTENTS

Contents

TEN YEARS

A NOMAD

INTRODUCTION

Getting the Bug

I haven't been everywhere, but it's on my list.

—SUSAN SONTAG

I AM A NOMAD.

For a decade I have lived a long, peripatetic life on the road. Three thousand nights.

In more than ninety countries. In a thousand different cities. In hundreds of hostels. With countless people. For half a million miles on airplanes, and half a million more (I've added it up) on trains and buses and tuk-tuks and cars and bicycles.

That was my home.

In all that time, over all those miles, I wandered with no goal. I wasn't on a trip, vacation, or pilgrimage. I had no list of set destinations or set sights to see. My only purpose was to travel. To be a nomad: Someone who could move from place to place without urgency, without plans. Someone whose destination was the journey itself. Someone who just picked up and went wherever and whenever they pleased.

Traditionally, nomads—whether in the deserts of the Middle East, on the steppes of Eurasia, or on the plains of North America—were born into an ancient practice of living life in motion. They were my role models, but unlike them, I wasn't born to travel, and had no tradition to draw from.

In my family, we didn't travel. My dad did the hippy thing after college, sleeping in German wheat fields and partying around Europe, but by the time my younger sister and I were born, my father's long hair had disappeared right along with any wanderlust he or my mom had. Instead, life became defined by the nine-to-five cycle of work.

Like most modern American middle-class families, if we went anywhere it was because we were on *vacation*—leisure travel with a fixed start and end, tied to the calendar of the working year, centered more often than not around visiting relatives. We left home to visit relatives in Philadelphia on holidays or took long road trips to see my grandmother in Florida. We'd visit Disneyworld and Universal Studios; go bowling; and eat early dinners with my grandmother *Mimi*. Long car rides, nights at big chain hotels, and trips to theme parks were par for the course.

Like figures from a Norman Rockwell painting come to life, we traveled like middle-class Americans were *supposed* to travel. Predictably. Safely. And never for too long. There would be no backpacking trips, camping excursions, or jaunts to exotic destinations for us. We were not only not nomadic, we were *rooted*, in place and in custom.

And, as far as I knew, there was no other way to live.

In my mind, travel was a planned break from the rhythm of corporate life, the adult equivalent of being on school break. You worked hard and you treated yourself to an all-inclusive destination a short flight away, or spent your time away from the office in some relative's living room. You took just enough time off that you could muster the strength to go to work every ordinary weekday for decades until it was time for that fabled thing called retirement, when life could truly begin.

Life had a specific path you were supposed to follow: grade school, secondary school, college, work, marriage, retirement.

After you had paid your dues and followed the rules then you were free to do anything you wanted.

I carried that impression of life and travel with me through my teenage years and into my early twenties. When I finished college, I dutifully and happily took my rightful place at the bottom of the middle-class corporate ladder, and took an entry-level job at a hospital in Boston. I answered phones, stocked and ordered supplies, and told visitors which room their sick relative was in—I did every job you'd expect of someone with no experience.

My life became full of routine.

Commute. Work. Thirty-minute lunch break. Gym with the roommate after work. Take out for dinner. TV before bed. On the weekends, my friends and I would try to meet girls at a bar. Each day blended seamlessly into another.

But this routine gnawed at my soul. I wasn't happy. I grew restless.

I felt as if I was watching my life from the outside, waiting for it to start. Life was supposed to start after college, right? Sure, everyone said that college represented the best years of their lives, but to me, it was always the "real world" that was supposed to be special.

The real world had things that college lacked: a place of my own; money; a steady relationship; the ability to go where I wanted; to do what I wanted; freedom. It was where I could finally start *my* life.

Except the real world turned out to be boring as hell.

It was my life, all right, and it turned out to be an endless loop of sameness. When I complained, I was often told that it was normal. How it's supposed to be. "Don't worry, honey. When you find a job you love, life will be a lot different," my mother would say to me. "You just graduated. You're twenty-three. Don't be so impatient. We all start off at the bottom."

As I approached my one-year anniversary at the hospital, my boss reminded me that I had to take my accrued vacation time soon. "It's policy," she said, "or you're going to lose it."

I can no longer remember how it happened—time has taken that precious memory, but I started thinking about Costa Rica. I had come across a tour in one of my many searches online. It wasn't anywhere I had been before, or had even thought much about prior to this, but it was certainly the kind of place my parents wouldn't have gone, which made it immediately attractive.

It looked . . . different. And I wanted different. Anything that wouldn't be filled with dreaded routine. An exotic locale where adventure—and maybe some danger—lurked. Online I saw photos of people on a beach, hiking in jungles, and spotting monkeys and exotic birds. They were on ziplines and surfboards. Things I had never done in my life. They were young. They were happy. But, more important than that, they looked far away from where I was, in that work break room, eating my microwaved lunch, fretting about the long commute home through the harsh Boston winter, which only served to remind me that I was stuck firmly at the bottom of the corporate hierarchy.

When I got home that night, I booked a tour to Costa Rica. I thought it was just going to be my first grown-up *vacation*.

It ended up being my first step toward something more than that.

⊕

I DON'T PRETEND MY STORY IS UNIQUE. Many, many people can tell a story like mine—because many, many people have found that the endless loop of commuting and ladder-climbing and evenings in front of the TV (or whatever their culture's version of that endless loop is) is not enough to satiate their being. Like me, they left; and, like me, they never came back—at least, not for a good, long while; and never the same as when they left.

The story of travel is a timeless tale. My fears and struggles and dreams have been feared and struggled and dreamt many times before—and, no doubt, will be many times after I am gone.

But I want to tell you my version anyway. I want to tell you the things I haven't told anyone else and that most travel writers seem afraid to say about what spending extended time traveling is *really* like.

1

Stepping Out the Door

He who is outside his door has the hardest part of the journey behind him.

—FLEMISH PROVERB

DO YOU EVER HOPE FOR AN EPIPHANY? That supposed moment of revelation or insight—the kind that happens near the end of a story where everything makes sense. In the story, the hero has struggles and doubts, and then something—it could be as small as the sight of a bird's nest in a tree or snow falling from the sky—happens that clarifies everything. Suddenly, everything in the hero's life seems to make sense. The hero has figured it out. They're a changed person. And because the thing that set it off is so seemingly insignificant, the implication is that *your* moment of epiphany is out there waiting for you, in the ordinary things that you take for granted.

You could change—*really* change—tomorrow.

It's a nice belief, right?

But life doesn't work like that.

We change all the time. The you you are now is different than the you from ten years ago, and the you in ten years will be different still. But the thought that we can pinpoint that change to a single, story-ready moment is something out of fiction. "Aha" moments are a rarity. Learning and change—even mind-altering learning and radical change—aren't spontaneous, and don't happen all at once. Only with distance, as we look back at the narrative of our existence, can we tell there was a moment when our old self disappeared, and a new person emerged, with new eyes and perspective. But even that moment wasn't when the change occurred, it was simply when we first notice it. This is the nature of evolution. Gradual, imperceptible change that accumulates over time until our first memory bears no resemblance to what we are looking at in present day.

That's how it was for me. I didn't become a nomad the day I booked my Costa Rica trip. It wasn't as if I was Corporate Matt, and then my first day standing beneath a jungle waterfall a few weeks later, I became Nomadic Matt. When I planned the trip, there was no sense that I was also planning to change my life, that my trip would be the first step to a rejection of nearly everything and everyone I had ever known. I had no idea I was setting in motion a journey that would not end, perhaps ever, and would cost me the price of a nice house in the suburbs, kicking my way from city to city, country to country, hostel to hostel; into, onto, and through more museums, excursions, bus trips, and food stalls than I can even remember.

I was nowhere near that fearless.

All I wanted was a vacation. Those two weeks to get me through the next fifty.

As I boarded a flight from Boston to San José, Costa Rica, near the end of April 2003, I was petrified. Going to Costa Rica with a small tour group was the safest "riskiest" thing I could do. I wasn't interested in a new life—I just wanted to go on some hikes, see some waterfalls and volcanoes, hang out on the beach, and make it home in one piece. Simple. Easy. Safe.

All of that other stuff—the freedom, the adventure, the possibility—the things that make you fall in love with travel lay in the future.

⊕

EXITING BAGGAGE CLAIM in San José, my eyes darted left and right. As I made my way into the arrivals area, taxi drivers pounced on me. I was fresh meat. It couldn't have been more obvious to them if I was hanging upside from a hook in a shop window. They spoke with such rapidity that my high school Spanish couldn't comprehend a syllable.

"Necesitas un taxi? A donde vas? Taxi? Taxi? Taxi?"

"No I don't want a ride. Uhhhhh . . . *No me gusta,*" I said trying to remember the right words. *"Yo tengo un* . . . driver. . . . No, no *necesito un taxi."*

The unfamiliarity. The discomfort. The entire experience was overwhelming.

I looked around for someone with a sign with my name. My tour came with an optional airport pickup and, if I had learned anything from my parents, the most important part of any trip was responsibly navigating airport logistics. Check into the flight the night before. Get to the airport early. *The airline says two hours before for international flights, let's make it three just in case there is traffic.* Pack your pillow and snacks for the plane. Find the cheapest rental car or the freest shuttle. *Whatever you do, don't get ripped off.*

In spite of me having spent God knows how many hours trying to avoid even the possibility of uncertainty upon arrival, my driver was nowhere to be found. With my heart racing and my palms sweaty, I paced around the arrivals hall, the tropical humidity only adding to my anxiety, absurd visions of spending my vacation trapped in the airport dancing in my head.

"Come on taxi real cheap," said a man approaching me.

"No," I said, sure that the invitation into the backseat of his taxi was an obvious ploy to kidnap and ransom me. *Why had I done this? What was I thinking? I can't do this.* Even if this man defied all the Central American stereotypes bouncing around my cloistered New Englander mind, how would I even know that he was taking me in the right direction? It's not like I knew these roads.

The foreignness of where I was suddenly hit me like a boxer landing an uppercut on his unsuspecting opponent. Even in something as universal as an airport—with a layout like every other airport—I was still in foreign place. Even an airport was a different experience.

As I entertained the thought of calling off the trip *(Maybe I was in over my head.)*, there in the back, standing near a pole, was my driver casually holding a sign with my name on it. Staring into space, he looked like he didn't care one way or the other if I actually showed up.

"I'm Matt," I said as I walked over him.

"Okay, *vamos*," he replied, grabbing my bag and ushering me to his dilapidated car.

In better days, the driver's car might have been a nice Toyota. Now, the sun-bleached blue paint was peeling to reveal a Swiss-cheesed rust finish. Inside, the fabric was equally worn. The floor was littered with trash and old soda cans. I don't know what I was expecting from my ride, but this definitely wasn't it.

As we pulled onto the highway, the nervous anxiety turned into pride. I had passed my first test. I had navigated the airport and found my ride! It was a small victory but it was *my* victory. Now, I was *here*. Settling into the threadbare backseat, I looked out the window and got my first glimpse of Costa Rica. There were cloud-covered mountains in the distance and banana fields as far as the eye could see. The blue sky was dotted with enough white, puffy clouds to make Bob Ross feel right at home.

But the pride (and the visions of a tropical paradise) quickly faded away as small houses with corrugated roofs and bars on their windows began to dot the highway into San José. I could see tiny dirt roads filled with potholes and trash strewn everywhere. Was *this* a shantytown?

As we entered San José, more homes sealed like prisons popped up, squished together on streets with run-down buildings and trash. With a burst of embarrassment, I remembered the manicured, middle-class suburb where I grew up. I'd been sheltered. I'd never seen anywhere this impoverished. I'd never had to navigate a road that was more pothole than road, or watch out for piles of trash littering the pavement as I walked. Boarded-up houses were reserved for the "bad" side of town, the side privileged kids like me stayed away from unless we were trying to get back at our parents or seem cool to our friends.

And just like that, all of the ugly stereotypes of Central America I'd absorbed from the news media over the previous two decades leapt to the forefront of my mind: crime; guerillas; drug cartels; kidnapping; disease. I was raised to be afraid of places like this—"places to be avoided"—and now that lesson was bubbling back to the surface.

What the hell was I doing here? And where is this guy really taking me?
I was alone in a foreign country, in a car with a guy I didn't

know, who spoke a language I didn't speak, and I had no idea where we were headed. This was not smart. This was not normal. This was not safe. *This is why people don't leave the country.*

"Aqui," the driver suddenly said, the third and final word in our entire exchange, his car and the escalating narrative in my head coming to a screeching halt at once. I was jolted back to reality and looked out the car window.

I had been so worried about "what ifs" that I missed the change in scenery. The neighborhood had changed. The homes were bigger, the roads were paved, the nearby park pristine, the streets clean. We were in front of a beautiful Spanish-style hotel. The scenery matched the expectations in my mind. And, to my young, inexperienced, sheltered self, that made me feel safer and reassured.

Okay, I thought to myself, *maybe I was too quick to judge. This doesn't seem bad at all.*

The driver dropped my bag in the hotel lobby and left without a word. I didn't even have a chance to tip him.

I gave my name to the front desk attendant, who scanned a sheet in front of him.

"Ahhh yes, excellent! Pura Vida!" he said, looking up with a smile. "Welcome to Costa Rica! Here's your key. Everything is all set! This is the note from your tour leader." He pointed to a sign on the desk that told us to enjoy our first day and to be back at 6:00 PM for a welcome meeting.

I walked to my room and saw another bag there. My roommate was already here. His leather backpack, the collared shirts neatly hung in the closet, the brown shoes laid out near the door, all spoke of a confidence that I was sorely lacking. He clearly wasn't worried about the possibility of making a mad dash for the airport in the middle of the night because of a coup.

Sitting on my bed, I took a deep breath. I grew up a nerd. The kind that played *Magic: The Gathering*, D&D, and read *Les Misérables* (the unabridged version) for fun. I had been waiting for a growth spurt since I entered high school, but it stood me up at prom and at graduation, too. Even among my friends, I felt un-cool. A nerd to the nerds, the one that got called last to hang out.

I brought the awkward nerdy voice in my head to college with me, so it didn't matter how good my grades were, how much better my friends were. I still didn't feel like I fit in. College was supposed to be a fresh start, but it never felt as if I was making much progress at creating a new, better me. There had been three other Matts in my residence hall, and I was the shortest out of all three (one was a basketball player). Suddenly, on the first day no less, I was known as "Mini-Matt." That's not a name you ever—*ever*—want to have. It was like a video game where you mess up early and know immediately that the whole rest of your turn is fucked. Better to just die and start over. My chance to reimagine my life was gone before I ever had a chance.

As freshman year ended, I hit the reset button and transferred to another school. *If I could just go somewhere new,* I thought, *somewhere with fewer Matts, I could start again and define myself before others defined me. That would solve all my problems. All I needed was a fresh start and then I'd be able to write my own story from page one.*

New clothes. New haircut. New me. *I am THE Matt here.*

At the University of Massachusetts Amherst, I joined a fraternity, became social chair, developed a large network of friends, starting dating, and grew into my own skin. People just called me Matt. I learned to fake confidence. But faking confidence is different from owning it. Faking it didn't get rid of the kid who felt like he looked like somebody's younger brother. The one people didn't really want to hang out with. The runt. Now, in a room four thousand miles from home, with a roommate I didn't choose, I worried the next ten days was going to be high school and college (tries one and two) all over again.

Patterns like this are hard to break. We're afraid of being hurt so we don't let anyone get close enough to hurt us. I didn't realize it at the time, but this was my first chance to connect with a fellow traveler, to meet someone new on the road, and already I was fitting him into the old patterns of my life. Before we even exchanged a word, I was processing him through a lens colored by fear, anxiety, and rejection. It was, I understand now, the way I reacted to most new people. How long until they saw through my thin veneer of self-confidence? How long until they discovered the nerd underneath?

At the same time, the experience of transferring to a new college gave me a different pattern. I could, if I wanted to, write my own story. After all, nobody on this trip knew me. Of course, travel isn't like going to a new college. Much less is familiar. Much more is uncomfortable. And because there are so many fewer points of reference from your old life, you have that much more freedom in crafting a new one.

The unfamiliarity of travel jolts you out of your familiar patterns. Who we are on the road is *different* from who we are at home. I don't know if who we are on the road is closer to our real self than who we are at home—having changed so much in my life, I'm not sure if the idea of a real self is all that useful, honestly. But I can say that being on the road gave me the opportunity to stop faking confidence and start building it; to stop acting like a new person and to start becoming one.

⊕

IN COSTA RICA, I could create my own story free from the baggage of home. I didn't know anyone's past. They didn't know mine. Our lives back home didn't matter. No one cared. All that mattered was how we acted then and there.

And, if it didn't work out? Who cared! I'd never see these people again anyways!

We all have an image of our ideal self in our minds. From the person who is a musical genius or can command an audience to the person who runs every day, tells witty jokes, reads a lot, or walks with confidence. In our minds, that ideal self is just being held back by the version of us who exists in everyday life. The one who justifies and rationalizes *why* you aren't your ideal self and why you keep failing.

But in Costa Rica, those justifications and rationalizations melted away. I had a blank slate to be whoever I wanted. I could be the ideal funny me. I could wake up and say to myself, "What would funny, confident Matt do?" without worrying if people would go, "Hey that's not the real you!" No one knew the real me. No one knew my shyness. My nerdiness. My insecurities. They just knew the now me, and as long as he was up for anything and didn't act like a jerk, my fellow travelers were more than ready to start new friendships. Because they were in the exact same place I was—experimenting with their new selves, their fun, outgoing travel selves.

Funny, confident Matt took his first big swing when the group moved to Arenal, a small town in central Costa Rica renowned for its lake, hot springs, caving, a gigantic waterfall, and a volcano of the same name. At breakfast one morning, I asked two of the women in our group if they wanted to go hiking after lunch. I was not a hiker. I was not the kind of person who walked up to two strangers, even if we had become friendly over the prior week, and asked them to do anything, let alone hike. To my surprise, they said yes.

Later that afternoon, we took a taxi to the entrance of Arenal Volcano National Park and headed into the jungle, which often quickly thinned out to rocky trails spreading out like spider veins from the side of the mountains. These were remnants of eruptions long past. We wandered off trail and down gravel paths, seeing where they led for the sake of the discovery itself. I felt like Indiana Jones. I jumped over rocks and climbed boulders, got my new friends to take photos of me, followed unknown local birds as they flew around, and, eventually, got us very lost.

We wanted to reach the lake on the western side of the volcano in time for sunset, and nothing on our map was helping us find our way there. In my defense, the trail map our hotel provided was simple and very vague. It showed the "official" trail, but its many nameless tributaries were poorly marked—if they were even marked at all. Most of the time we weren't even totally sure which trail we were on. Funny, confident Matt told himself this was all part of the fun of new travel adventures. Which it was, until the sun started to set.

Every trail we took, every bit of direction we got from hikers we passed seemed just to send us deeper into the forested slopes of the volcano. We went down trails that ended abruptly. We doubled back, found new trails, and the best we could do was go around in circles. As the sky turned a deep pink overhead, and day turned into night, mosquitoes began to hunt us by the scent of our sweat and animals came out of the brush to scavenge, no longer scared off by a thousand hiking tourists.

Then our flashlights died. In the creeping darkness, the three of us took turns using the light from our camera screens to illuminate our crappy map and divine the way back to the main road. With each false start my anxiety spiked and the trepidation within the group increased. I don't remember who figured it out, or how, but finally we found our way to a dirt road that connected to the main highway. Roads meant cars. Cars meant people. People meant a way back.

When we got to the highway, it was empty. There were no cars. Tired and hungry, we began the long walk back to the hotel in silence. The whole way I worried that these two kind, trusting women would never talk to me again. Thankfully, before I could go too far down this spiral, a car appeared over the ridge behind us and slowed to a crawl when the driver spotted us along the side of the road. He stopped and asked if we needed a lift. Without a second thought, the three of us piled into the backseat. A week before I had been uncertain of how to get from the airport to the hotel, I had been terrified to get into anything that wasn't an officially sanctioned tour bus and now I was hitchhiking.

As the driver pulled away, each of us turned to look at the mountain and watch it glow red as lava oozed down the side. It was the first moment in hours that any of us had stopped to appreciate the beauty that had brought us out on this hike in the first place. It was other-worldly. Instantly, our mood lifted. I'd had more excitement in half a day than I'd had in my entire life up to that point. And even more, I had a story. *We had a story. A shared experience.* One that bound us as travelers.

IN MY LIFE BACK HOME, I could plan out my days months in advance. I knew where every week would take me. There was no mystery, no "what's around the next bend?" I'd wake up, get ready for work, commute, work, take a lunch, work again, commute home, make dinner, watch TV, vow to *finally* hit the gym tomorrow, and repeat for five days. There was little variation to that—maybe a happy hour, movie, or dinner here or there. On weekends, I ran errands.

Costa Rica was the opposite. Every day was unplanned, exciting, and adventurous. I was doing anything I wanted, making friends from around the world, and pushing myself to the limit. It was liberating. There was no judging. No baggage. Nothing I did before I came on the tour mattered—all that mattered was living in the moment with these new friends. After Arenal, we hiked more mountains, saw dolphins, ziplined, came up close to wildlife, went caving, explored tropical jungles. I took part in every activity. No opportunity was wasted.

Costa Rica showed me a world without commutes or days that blended seamlessly together, days when you didn't wear shoes for hours at a time, where you talked to strangers and got lost. Every day was so different I sometimes wondered if I hadn't lived three lifetimes by the time I fell asleep in bed. Days seemed to stretch endlessly and warp my perception of time. We did so much that places we visited the day before felt like they were years ago. Time did not drag like at home but slowed down to let so much happen that it stretched endlessly.

It stood in sharp contrast to the routine-filled life I had come to know back home. Now, I had seen a world where routine didn't have to exist. That was the beauty of travel. Now I saw why people loved to go on vacation and always talked so highly of their trips to strange, far-off places. You could break free from everything! I was breaking free from my routine, but also from the version of myself I had grown tired of and the assumptions about what kind of person I had to be. For the first time, I felt like I was in the driver's seat of my own life. I was the person I always thought I could be. I finally got it.

I was addicted to the high.

I wanted more.

2

Taking the Leap

*The whole object of travel is not to set foot on foreign land;
it is at last to set foot on one's own country as a foreign
land.*

— G. K. CHESTERTON

THE PLANE TOUCHED DOWN in Boston without incident. I followed the signs to baggage claim, listened to the announcements over the PA system ("safety is everyone's concern"). Everything was in English. Everything was legible, familiar, easy.

I was home.

It was as if I could feel my senses fading back to their ordinary dullness, my body and mind preparing itself for more cycles of the endless routine. It was amazing how quickly it all happened. By the time I got into my roommate's car, Costa Rica was a memory and the force of decades of habit reasserted itself.

I unlocked my apartment, flipped on the lights, opened the windows to air the place out. This is where I sit on the couch. This is where I have hot showers. This is where I go to sleep and wake up to start all over again. It was like in *Fight Club,* "I loved every stick of furniture in that place." I had painstakingly picked out every piece of it from Ikea, and now I was repulsed by the sight of them. If I closed my eyes, I could see the cycle going around and around, spinning out for months and years into the future. And, like a counterweight to all that weight of anticipated routine, I found myself thinking—in the shower, on my commute, at my desk, on the couch I had assembled myself—of *elsewhere.*

This mythical place became the focus of all my desires. *Elsewhere* was anywhere but answering the office phone, filling out paperwork, restocking shelves, or staring at my computer. It was a place of foreign lands and cultures, of laughing with new friends in cafés, of hiking, discovery, freedom, and unencumbered possibility.

It was one thing to spend my time entering data into spreadsheets before I knew that there was something better out there, but now that Costa Rica had awakened this new desire in me, it became much harder to persist through the drudgery.

Whereas before I was asleep, now I was awake.

Now that I knew there was somewhere else where other somebodies lived—or at least spent way more than a week's vacation—getting to that place was all I really wanted to think about. Elsewhere.

That was where I belonged.

In the space of a few short weeks, the corporate ladder that I was supposed to be thankful for having a place (at the bottom) on had turned into a StairMaster. A machine that went in an endless loop, and could actually make you stronger if you let it, but only at one thing: staying on the machine for longer and longer stretches.

Awakening to the idea that you belong somewhere else is a recipe for wanderlust. It's also how you become really crappy at your job and look for ways to get the hell out of there as soon as you can.

A better world was out there—and I had to get there fast.

During my downtime at work, I daydreamed. I researched trips. I read travel books. I kept myself visually elsewhere as I watched my holiday time slowly accrue back up. I ticked down the months until the calendar would change again and I could race out of the office and toward a plane like a kid on the last day of school.

IN 2005, as soon as the year ticked over and I could take another vacation, I found a friend, picked a place, and left as soon as possible.

The friend was Scott, the place was Bangkok (to start), and our departure was January. *Early* January.

My elsewhere had arrived.

Thailand was going to be different than Costa Rica. There would be no guided tours in Thailand. No resorts. No prechosen roommates. *Elsewhere* couldn't be purchased in a package like that.

I had done the tour thing and felt, with a friend, I could easily travel unaided by a guide. I had cut my chops. I was ready to go pro.

On our first morning in Bangkok, we decided to hire a boat to take us up and down the Chao Phraya River. We wanted to check out one of the floating markets that, according to the internet, Southeast Asian river cities were famous for.

Simple enough. Until we got into a taxi outside our hotel. First and foremost, the taxis in Bangkok didn't have meters—which meant we were at the mercy of the driver and whatever price he felt like naming at the end of the trip. And when he overheard what we were planning for the day, we were at his mercy once more because he took matters into his own hands and drove us to his friend who he promised would offer us a "great deal" on a river cruise—floating market included.

If there was a great deal to be had, we weren't the beneficiaries of it. The floating market we were taken to wasn't really a market at all. It was a tourist trap, populated by nothing more than a few locals selling trinkets to people like me. Scott and I sat there being badgered by vendors for what seemed like an eternity, locked in a stalemate with our boatman who wanted us to buy something and who we wanted to keep going. Finally, after seeing we would buy nothing, he blinked, and turned the boat around.

Back ashore, feeling down from our first failed attempt at independent travel, we followed the guidebook to the Grand Palace, the former residence of the royal family. Though no longer used except for royal ceremonies and state visits, the palace was the main tourist attraction in the city with its numerous temples, statues, reliefs, and buildings. We came upon the palace's large walls that hid all but the top of the magnificent temples that loomed within.

Yet there wasn't a soul around, and the giant doors in front of us were closed.

"It's closed for lunch. It will open again at 2:00 PM," said a Thai guy strolling over to us. "I can take you to some other temples in the meantime. Cheap price!"

Scott and I were still wary from the boat scam, but with the Grand Palace doors shut and no one else around, going somewhere seemed like a better option than just sitting there and going nowhere.

We got in the man's tuk-tuk and sped down a side street and into traffic. Cars were at a standstill in traffic, but motorbikes weaved in and out of them, while the tuk-tuks cut off both trying to change lines. The stop-and-start of it all allowed us to take in a part of the city we hadn't seen yet. The sidewalks were filled with vendors and food stalls that overflowed into traffic, there was trash littering the road, and an odor that I didn't know pollution could have. It was an assault on all the senses—including common sense. Something didn't feel right. I opened up my guidebook and found a section on temple tour scams. Fuck. We did it again.

Looking up at driver, I told him "No shops. We just want to visit the temples."

"Yes," he said smiling into the rearview mirror. "Only temples! No shopping!"

But of course he took us shopping—exactly as our book said he would, and exactly as we could have predicted if either of us had bothered to read it on the plane. Every temple he did take us to (and he took us to quite a few), was always just around the corner from some shop he knew. First, there was a gem shop (just a quick look he said), then the souvenir shop, and then a suit shop.

I was able to stay strong, but Scott finally gave in and bought a suit. Once the transaction was complete, our tour abruptly ended. I realized in retrospect, the whole thing was much more scripted than serendipitous—the shops hired our driver to bring in unwitting Western customers, who were much more likely to be enticed by promises of a "temple tour" than a "shopping trip nobody asked for." Once a mark bought something—and that's exactly what we were, marks—he made his money and he was done with us.

We piled into the man's tuk-tuk and he drove us straight back to the Grand Palace. There would be no other palaces or temples on this "tour."

Looking around as he dropped us off, I noticed that something was different. This wasn't the same plaza as before. There was a big field behind us now. And lots of buildings. Then it clicked.

The reason we couldn't find the entrance earlier was because we'd been at the *back* of the palace. Had we walked around, we would have found that it was open. Our driver was smart enough to know that—and smart enough to take us down a side street to keep us from seeing the entrance.

That tricky sonuvabitch.

In my childhood days of family road trips and theme park visits, scams like these were spoken of in tones of horror—a scam was the worst thing that could happen to the upstanding tourist.

Yet I had been scammed—*twice*—on my first day.

With time, one comes to realize that if you don't occasionally get scammed on your travels, you aren't pushing yourself enough. Scams happen to confused people in unfamiliar places, people who don't take preapproved tours and deviate from their guidebooks. Going to unfamiliar places and getting a bit lost was exactly the *elsewhere* I was looking for, even if that meant taking on some risks. Of course, I'd never recommend letting your guard drop completely and putting yourself in a situation of real danger. But most scam artists are like the guy on the tuk-tuk—someone trying to wring a few bucks out of a tourist to feed his family. A bit dishonest, but basically harmless. If you don't occasionally run into someone like that, you're traveling in a bubble. Or you're not even traveling at all—you're vacationing.

Scams, in a way, keep you growing. They help you suss out the intentions of those around, make you learn from your mistakes—and remind you to stop making the same ones.

My real goal—and I wasn't nearly there yet—was to get beyond the stage where scams were around every corner and to put myself into off-the-guidebook situations while still keeping my wits about me. It was, to say the least, a work in progress.

I had started the day a pro but, by the end, I was reminded I was still an amateur with a lot to learn. The world has a funny way of always keeping you in your place.

⊕

BANGKOK WAS, in its way, another new experience for me— the experience of disappointed expectations. When it came time to head north for Chiang Mai, we were more than happy to leave those dashed expectations behind us. Bangkok felt polluted and crowded, full of touts and smog and scams. We hoped the rest of Thailand would be better. After all, there *must* be a reason why millions visited the country every year. We were looking forward to smaller cities, jungle tours, and days lounging on the beach.

On our second day in Chiang Mai, I read about a temple located outside the city called Wat Phra Doi Suthep. It was Chiang Mai's most famous. The pagoda in its center supposedly contains relics of the Buddha himself, there are sweeping views of the surrounding countryside, monks lead public chanting, and there is an intricately carved 309-step staircase leading up to it.

Scott didn't want to go, so, not wanting to pass up possible adventure, I went on my own.

And, as I got into the bus to the temple—a converted pickup truck with wooden benches and a roof added to keep out the rain—the course of my life changed. Looking back, I can say that this was when the seed that was planted in Costa Rica came into full bloom. This was the moment when my life pivoted.

Inside the bus were five people: three Canadians, a couple and a third wheel who they met and developed a rapport with on the Thai island of Ko Chang (a paradise, I was told many times over); and a Belgian couple who were simply taking a month off work to escape the Brussels winter. We struck up a conversation.

Where are you from? How long are you traveling? Where have you been? What do you do?

These are all the typical questions travelers ask each other to form the foundation of a conversation and of commonality. We bond over the one thing we know we have in common: travel.

They were bewildered that I only got two weeks' vacation a year.

"So what will you do the rest of the year? You're just going to stay home?" they asked.

"I hadn't really thought about it." I shrugged. "I just wanted to get away now. I mean I get sick leave I could use for a trip but this is probably my only vacation for the year. I don't think I could afford another."

"Americans have the worst vacation policy," the solo Canadian traveler said in loathing.

"Well, I can save as much vacation time as I want, and could take longer if I got permission, but I doubt it'd be longer than three weeks and it could still only be about once a year. But that's assuming I don't get sick and have to use that time, too."

"I couldn't imagine only one holiday per year," said the male half of the Belgian couple. "We get two months in Belgium and most people also take August off. You shouldn't live to work. There's too much to see in the world. You must live your life."

As my new friends and I continued discussing travel, time off, and doing what you loved, I realized how uniquely American this phenomenon was.

These travelers talked about how no one else around the world did what we do. How no one else made, or would even think of making, that bargain. And they were right.

Americans trade time for money and, although we all complain about it, it's an arrangement we've kept in place for decades. Even as traveling and career breaks have become more mainstream, this fundamental arrangement has not changed. Taking extended time off is simply not part of our cultural norms—and I don't think it ever will be.

In my years on the road, I've met people from around the world, and none of their cultures make this tradeoff. Even the notoriously overworked Japanese have a more flexible holiday schedule than American workers. Even they travel in larger numbers than we do. Recent reports* state that close to half of Americans don't take vacation time! HALF!

So even when we are allowed to go, we don't.

Trundling up to this serene Buddhist temple on a rough wooden bench that was much less comfortable than the sofa I paid good money for back home in Boston, I began to see this

---

* https://www.ustravel.org/research/state-american-vacation-2018

tradeoff between time and money for what it truly was—a devil's bargain—and how unhappy it made me.

Had I really just used my entire year's vacation? What *would* I do the rest of the year? And how are these guys taking a year off? What would they do for money and work? What was their secret? Were they rich? Their lifestyle seemed as foreign as the country we were riding through together, but I couldn't help be anything but envious of their freedom.

I wanted to be out living life and experiencing the world, not sitting behind a desk. To me, life felt like it happened when you traveled. There you were an active participant. It was on the road that I felt most at ease, most alive, and, most importantly, happy.

As I toured the temple and went to bed that night, their words and ideas hung over me like a cloud.

The next day, Scott and I took a cooking class—and found the three Canadians in it. As if the universe was trying to tell me something. Fate had brought us together again and now was my chance to get all my questions answered. There, in the kitchen of a little restaurant as we (poorly) made Pad Thai and spicy curry, I peppered them with the questions about their lifestyle that had played over and over again in my head the night before.

How did you save money?

We worked and used our savings to fund our trip. We might work on the road and take odd jobs to extend it. There's actually a lot of ways to earn money when you travel, but since Southeast Asia is so cheap, we don't need to do that right now.

What about your parents? What did they think?

Our parents only get upset if we forget to call every couple weeks.

Yeah, but is this safe?

You have to worry about being ripped off and scammed, but I haven't felt physically unsafe. People are generally good people. You Americans tend to view the world as this fundamentally dangerous place, but it's not.

What about planning? I mean, how do you plan for this?!

You just learn to go with the flow. We planned a lot in the beginning but then you keep changing plans. You like a place and stay longer, or hate a place and leave. We usually decide a few days before we want to go somewhere that we'll be there.

Do you speak the local languages? Is it hard to get around?

Nope. But people speak enough English where you can get by. Pointing helps.

How do you stay on budget? Do you plan everything?

Traveling isn't really that expensive. You eat local food, stay in cheap guesthouses, take local transportation. I'm barely spending any money here. Beer is my biggest expense, especially when compared to Canada. I mean, a meal is less than a dollar.

What happens if you get sick? What about your future? What about work?

Dude, doctors exist all over the world. This isn't 1700. You can buy medicine anywhere you need. Okay, maybe not in the jungles of Africa, but definitely here in Thailand. And the future? Who knows? Life is what happens when you're making other plans. We'll worry when we move back to Canada.

I listened, wide-eyed, to their answers as they became my heroes.

They seemed to have unlocked a secret to travel I didn't know existed. The more they told me about their lifestyle—meeting people around the world, living in bungalows on the beach, eating delicious and cheap food, taking local transportation, and endless sightseeing—the more envious I became. They were living *my* dream, while I was just on a temporary break from the time-honored American tradition of working to live. They were masters of their domain while I was just using up my vacation days.

I wanted to experiment with that life for myself—to try it and see if I could really make it mine. So after Chiang Mai, I made Scott stay one night on Bangkok's Khoa San Road. It is ground zero for the backpacker scene in Southeast Asia. I wanted to test out what being a backpacker was like. I wanted to play the part and see if it fit. To fake it and see if I could make it.

At a bar that night, I imagined myself as Backpacker Matt—someone who lived out of his backpack, someone who was brave and adventurous and always on the road, someone who had no problems striking up conversations with strangers. I walked up to a girl I'd never met before and invited her over to our table for drinks—something I'd never in a million years have done at home.

I could really do this, I thought the next day as Scott and I left Bangkok again. I could stay in run-down hostels, eat cheap street food, talk to strangers, and have the adventure of my life. Or more simply, just *have* a life.

⊕

IT'S OFTEN SAID THAT the point of travel isn't merely to see new places, but to see your old place in a new way. I was seeing Thailand, just as I'd seen Costa Rica, but more importantly, I was coming to see what my own home looked like as a foreign country. From Thailand, and in the company of my new heroes, my life looked much smaller than I had imagined. I had grown up with the notion that America was the best place on earth. The biggest, the richest, the freest, the most important—the "shining city on a hill." Things happened outside our borders, but everyone outside those borders looked longingly to America. We were the model for everything and everyone else.

And, within that American bubble, there was another bubble, the one in which I lived my $30,000 annual salary life. It was, we told ourselves, the best way of life in the best country on earth: the path from school to job to home ownership to retirement, with a couple of weeks of travel (to Disneyworld, most likely) sprinkled in each year. That *was* life. It was the life all other lives were aspiring to. The American Dream.

But here, in Thailand, were people who didn't want to live that life at all. People who were happy to be from somewhere other than America. People who believed, and acted as if, life was for *living*—not planning, saving, and climbing up to the next rung. It wasn't about working until you retired so you could then start your life.

It was about living it right now.

The most remarkable thing, though, was how *normal* these people seemed. These were not cult members or drugged-out hippies. They were fundamentally ordinary people making the best of the time they were given. They were doing fine.

Why wouldn't I also be fine? I was an able-bodied adult.

The earth has been host to nomadic cultures for as long as we have records—certainly for thousands of years, but likely much, much longer. Nomads have often butted heads with their "civilized" neighbors: civilizations build walls, while nomads travel with the changing seasons; civilizations keep livestock fenced in, while nomads follow herds across the plains or the steppe.

But while I've tried to borrow a basic ethos from nomads across history—never stop moving—there's an important way in which the modern nomad is a wholly different creature. True nomads travel for the sake of their livelihood, for subsistence and food.

I wanted to travel to experience the world.

I think that's also the case for some of the most famous travelers in human history whose names we know. I think of people like the Muslim voyager Ibn Battuta, who journeyed from Morocco to China in the middle ages as a pilgrim, a trader, and an official. Or someone like Zheng He, the great admiral who explored the Pacific and Africa on behalf of the Chinese emperor in the 1400s.

I'm inspired by them and the likes of Francesco Petrarca (better known as Petrarch), because he came up with a crazy idea: traveling for no reason at all. Petrarch was an Italian poet in the 1300s. The short encyclopedia entry on him is that he's basically one of the reasons we had the Renaissance. One day in 1336, Petrarch, his brother, and two servants decided to climb a mountain—Mont Ventoux, in the south of France. That probably doesn't sound like an especially big deal, but in the 1300s people didn't climb mountains, they overcame them, to get somewhere else. Mountains were something in the way. They were steep, dangerous, cold, rocky. People even described them as "ugly." And in a way, they were—they were obnoxious things that kept you from doing what you wanted to do, and getting where you wanted to go.

And this is why Petrarch's idea was so crazy: he wanted to climb a mountain just to see the view from the top. He didn't have any business to do or money to make on the other side of the mountain, and there wasn't a religious shrine or pilgrimage site on the way. He set out to climb a mountain for the hell of it. And he says (with some exaggeration, but probably not much) that he is the first one to even think of recreational mountain-climbing since ancient times.

His ascent of Mont Ventoux is described in a letter, which is one of the most famous pieces of writing—travel writing, in fact—to come out of that time. Petrarch writes:

> To-day I made the ascent of the highest mountain in this region, which is not improperly called Ventosum. My only motive was the wish to see what so great an elevation had to offer. I have had the expedition in mind for many years; for, as you know, I have lived in this region from infancy, having been cast here by that fate that determines the affairs of men. Consequently the mountain, which is visible from a great distance, was ever before my eyes, and I conceived the plan of some time doing what I have at last accomplished to-day.

Now Petrarch is playing up the drama a bit here. If you've ever been to the south of France and seen it, Mont Ventoux is not that fearsome. It's not even an Alp. Its top is about 6,000 feet above sea level (for comparison, the major peaks in the Rockies are at 14,000 feet), and you can get up and down in a day without any fancy mountaineering gear. The thing about Petrarch isn't that he had the superhuman strength to climb a mountain before anyone invented crampons and oxygen tanks—it's that he had the idea to climb a mountain. For the simple joy of it.

Petrarch and his party made it to the peak. Finally at the top, he was rewarded with a glorious view—a view that no human being had seen for centuries.

> At first, owing to the unaccustomed quality of the air and the effect of the great sweep of view spread out before me, I stood like one dazed. I beheld the clouds under our feet, and what I had read of Athos and

Olympus seemed less incredible as I myself witnessed the same things from a mountain of less fame. I turned my eyes toward Italy, whither my heart most inclined. The Alps, rugged and snow-capped, seemed to rise close by, although they were really at a great distance. . . .

Seven hundred years ago, it took a genius to imagine that travel was something you could do for no reason at all. You can just go see something because it exists. *That's* what appealed to me. *That's* the way I wanted to travel. The travelers I met showed me you don't have to be rich to get on a budget airline and go. You just need the same desire that Petrarch experienced: the desire to take in the view, to see just how much this wide world has to offer.

That's what I mean by the modern nomadic path. Some people travel because they have places to go. Others travel because the journey is their true home. They want to see and experience and live as much as possible in their short time on this earth.

In Thailand, I found that life was calling me. The idea that came into my head wasn't as new as it was when it came into Petrarch's, but it still felt like a discovery to me: you can—you should—travel for no reason at all.

⊕

ONE DAY, on the last stop of our trip, I left Scott to explore the island of Ko Samui, the island paradise with stunning beaches of white sand that have made Thailand so famous. I discovered a tiny sliver of sand with no resorts or restaurants called Lipe Noi beach. Local kids played in the sea. The soft pillowy clouds hung in the air over giant palm trees that shot out like claws to meet them. I could walk out seemingly forever in the water over flat, soft sand. I sat down in the water and gazed at the island behind me.

Was I really going to leave this all behind in a few days? Was I really going to spend another year in an office without another break, not just working for the weekend, like Loverboy sung, but toiling for those two weeks when I could finally get the hell out of there again? I felt my stomach knot as I thought about going back.

All I had desired since Costa Rica was to travel more— *elsewhere*—but it felt impossible.

Now, though, I felt like I found the answer to a question I didn't know I was asking. The cure to my unhappiness, my boredom, my lack of confidence wasn't anything I could find at home.

The cure was to keep traveling.

Backpacking was the lifestyle I had been searching for. It meant exposure to new cultures and new places and new foods. It meant forging instant friendships with strangers who had nothing in common with me but the same wanderlust. It meant ultimate freedom. It allowed me to take charge of my life instead of just merely watching the days and weeks and months waste away.

This was the life I wanted.

There on the beach I had my epiphany. I found that moment of clarity where I know what I had to do.

Or so one might say.

Looking back, I can trace my decision to quit my job and travel the world to that beach in Ko Samui but so much lead up to me being ready to make that decision. It had been slowly building—first in Costa Rica, then reinforced by my time back home at an unfulfilling job, then by the backpackers in Chiang Mai, and then by my experience on Khao San Road.

Each moment was another step forward that would have been impossible to take without the one before it.

On my last night in Ko Samui, I walked into the only English-language bookstore on the island and bought Lonely Planet's *Southeast Asia on a Shoestring*. I held it in my hand and I dreamed of all the places I could go. The guide, sealed in plastic wrap, symbolized my future.

When I was thumbing through the book at dinner, Scott wanted to know what I was doing with a new travel book for the very place we were just about to leave. I told him: I was going to go back home for just long enough to tie up my loose ends, and then pick up my journey again. I was going to quit my job, pack my bag, and travel for a year.

He didn't believe me, but my mind was made up.

I went back to reading the book, holding it as if it were an ancient holy book. A relic that contained hidden knowledge that I, a new initiate, had to decipher. It was my guide into the unknown. How could I stretch my money for a whole year? How could I get by without speaking a word of the language? How could I avoid getting scammed? How could I make my travel as rewarding as I imagined it would be? How could I do it as effortlessly as the new friends I met in Thailand? All of those answers, it seemed to me, were in this book.

Above all, I felt lifted up by the assurance that this adventure— this new path I had just discovered—was not going to end. I was not just going to be someone who went on vacation. I wasn't going to take a temporary break. Travel was going to become my identity—it was going to become who I was and what I lived for.

I was going to be a nomad.

3

The Pressures of Home

*Twenty years from now you will be more disappointed by the
things that you didn't do than by the ones you did do. So
throw off the bowlines. Sail away from the safe harbor. Catch
the trade winds in your sails. Explore. Dream. Discover.*

—H. JACKSON BROWN'S MOTHER

THE DECISION TO BLOW UP your life as you know it is often
met by the people around you in a few different ways.

While all I'd done by this point was buy a guidebook, that
guidebook was an ironclad commitment. Buying it, packing it
in my suitcase, and taking it home cemented my decision to
become a nomad. I was too stubborn to change my mind.
Breaking that promise to myself was not an option. Thailand
had changed me, and there was no going back. I knew this to
my core.

Even still, it took me weeks to work up the courage to tell my
friends and family. I sat on the idea, unsure what they would
say and how they would react. We crave the approval of the
people important in our lives, after all, and when it doesn't come
in our moments of greatest vulnerability, it can be crushing.

Would they encourage me and help me slay the negativity in my mind?

Or would they add to it?

It wasn't that I was wavering—it was just that I needed a little help, a little reassurance, a little, "I wish I had done that when I was your age. Godspeed."

I decided to tell my boss first.

He was a bald, heavyset, affable guy with a love for cooking and wine, who always encouraged me to strive for more. I figured he would be the most understanding and encouraging. And I owed it to him to give him plenty of time to find a replacement.

I was nervous about it. I had just transferred into this new role a few months ago and I felt like I was bailing on him, but once I walked into his office, shut the door, and sat down, I found the courage to lay it all out there. I told him about how ever since my Costa Rica trip I couldn't stop thinking about traveling. I told him about meeting my new Canadian and Belgian friends and how I knew from talking with them that I had to travel around the world before I started my career. And I told him that whatever career that might end up being, it wouldn't be in health care.

He leaned back in his large leather chair and gave me a dissatisfied look.

"You've only been here eight months, Matt. It's hard to find a new person, especially someone good. I think there's a future for you in health care."

As he spoke, I heard a mix of anger, sadness, and disappointment in his voice. He had taken to being my mentor, giving me more and more important tasks, letting me manage one of the training programs he was responsible for, and coaching me into adulthood. It wasn't simply that he'd have to go to the effort of replacing me—I really think he believed I had a future there.

"I won't leave right away," I replied. "I'll stay until July, finish my MBA, and then leave for my trip. That will give you six months to find a replacement."

"I had always seen you as a potential hospital executive or CEO one day."

It was flattering, if not also totally manipulative. Not a lot of entry-level employees get that sort of vote of confidence from their boss, assuming he really meant it. I choose to think he did. And what did it mean if I was right? A million-dollar-a-year salary. A big office. A staff. Fancy dinners. Attractive things. But would I bet my future happiness that they were really on the table? And would I want to spend the next twenty-five to thirty years of my life getting there?

I remembered my elsewhere. And I remembered the guidebook sitting in my desk.

"I appreciate it," I told him. "But I know this is the right thing for me right now. And the timing is perfect."

He sat there in silence, his face lost in thought as he processed the information. I grew more nervous as each second on the clocked ticked by.

He rubbed his head and sighed.

"Okay, I'll talk to the office manager and we'll start looking for your replacement. I'll miss you. But if you feel this is right, I think you should do it."

It was a hard conversation, but as I walked out, I realized that it went about as well as I could've hoped. He appreciated me enough to push me to stay; he understood me enough to accept that I wouldn't.

My parents? They were not as understanding.

"YOU ARE GOING TO WHAT?" they screamed in unison as I broke the news over dinner.

"Think this over a little more. What about your job? School? What will you do for the future?" said my mom.

"It's too late. I already quit my job."

"When did you do that?"

"Last week," I said.

They were dumbfounded

"Well, that was stupid," my dad said sternly. "Unquit it."

"I don't think it works that way, Dad."

"Why can't you just go to Europe like a normal person? What about safety? What about money? How will you stay in touch? Where are you going to go?" my mom continued, reciting every question I asked myself as I listened to my Canadian friends in Thailand describe their lives on the road

"Mom, I'm going to Europe. I'm also just going to all these other places, too. I met lots of travelers when I was in Thailand. They were fine."

Their list of concerns could have filled a library.

They were certain I was setting off toward certain death. They listed every natural disaster and political uprising they could think of. They reeled off facts about earthquakes and terrorists and coups like they were reading a deck of Trivial Pursuit cards designed to frighten children. But I held fast. I told them I loved them, that I would be fine, and that I would be sure to call them regularly from the road.

As for my friends, I imagined them taking this news incredibly well. That I'd share news of this amazing adventure and be bombarded with congratulations and admiration. "This guy," they would tell people, "he's off on an adventure of a lifetime." For once, I'd be the one who was envied.

But that was just a movie in my head. It was wish fulfillment. I hoped that doing something crazy would make me the most interesting man in the room. Instead, I learned that no one becomes interesting in a day. Being interesting is a quality you build up over the course of your experiences—not a quality you get by *planning* to have experiences.

Contrary to the movie in my head, my friends generally shrugged. "Oh, cool," was the general reply—and then they'd move on. I don't think they knew what to say. There was no frame of reference to point to. No friend, TV personality, celebrity, or social media star where they could say "Oh, just like so and so." What I was doing was so out of the norm—so far from their bubble—that the best reaction was indifference.

But their indifference hurt me more than my parents' outrage. I wanted to talk about this amazing life change I was planning, but everyone was more caught up in their own lives. No one wanted to hear about my planning, worries, itineraries, or my must-see list. If anything, they thought I was crazy for leaving a good job, wasting a new MBA and leaving with lots of new debt.

I learned that being interesting would be harder than making a single dramatic decision. More than that, there's a paradox about being "interesting." Just as confident people don't talk about how confident they are, and funny people don't tell you how hilarious they are, being interesting is not something interesting people aspire to. I've met my share of interesting people on the road—starting in that cooking class in Thailand—and what I thought of them was not something they were actively striving to cultivate. Rather, being interesting was a quality they carried with them; it was part of who they were, a character trait. It came out in the stories they told, in the way they carried themselves, in the confidence from pursuing a passion whether or not other people gave a damn.

Interesting people aren't interested in being interesting. They're deeply interested in some part of the world around them—in learning karate, or in brewing the perfect cup of coffee, or in watercolor painting, or in travel—and that passion rubs off on the people around them. Whatever it is, pursuing that passion weighs more heavily for them than, say, impressing friends or looking cool at parties.

⊕

SOCIETY USES SCRIPTS—PATTERNS OF action stored in our cultural memory—to make sense of the stories of our lives. We all understand, "I'm going off to college," or "I'm going on vacation"—those are culturally sanctioned ways of leaving your home. In the Middle Ages, the scripts were different— maybe "I'm going on a pilgrimage to the Holy Land"—but they served the same function. Pilgrims were recognizable figures. It's not necessarily that everyone knew one—but everyone knew *about* them, had read stories of them and seen depictions of them. They demonstrated what travel looked like; talking about them was a way of talking about what it meant to leave home.

But we can only fit so many of these scripts, these models of travel, into our heads at any given time. When we hear about a kind of travel that *doesn't* fit into them, it's as if we can't imagine it. We can't conceive of such a thing. Imagine using a time machine to teleport back to medieval England, strolling into the nearest marketplace, and announcing: "This summer, after everyone is done planting the crops, I am going to 'vacate' this town. I am going to borrow an oxcart and travel several hundred miles to the coast. When I get there, I am going to spread out a piece of fabric on the sand and sit on it. I will bring along a cask of ale to drink, and maybe I will hire a minstrel to sing me tales of great deeds while I am sitting on the sand on my piece of fabric. I am going to do this for two weeks. After that, my period of 'vacation' will be over, and I will reluctantly travel home."

I'm pretty sure the response to that would sound a lot like my parents' response to me: "YOU ARE GOING TO WHAT?"

I'd probably get burned at the stake.

That's how our mental scripts work. Only certain kinds of activities—travel, in this case—are allowed to fit into them. The rest are, by definition, crazy.

The problem is that, when I broke my news to the people close to me, there wasn't really a common script in 2004 for "I'm quitting my job to travel around the world." Of course, people did it. People had been doing it for centuries. Hippies popularized it to a degree. The Hippie Trail extended from Europe to India and beyond to Southeast Asia. But not enough people did what I was planning to do to make it an easily recognizable pattern in modern middle-class America. My friends didn't say much about my plans because they didn't know how to think about what I was doing. And it seems that some people, like my parents, reacted so negatively because I sounded like a crazy person.

My coworkers were no better. They too thought I was nuts.

"Why are you quitting your job? That's rash."

"The world isn't safe. Don't you read the news? Terrorists are everywhere!"

"What are you running away from that you're going to travel for so long?"

"You're an idiot for giving up a good job."

"You just finished school. What about your new degree? How are you going to pay for things?"

"I wish I could do that. It must be nice to not have any responsibility," they'd say sarcastically.

The list of criticisms from all quarters of my life went on and on, pretty much all the way up until it was time to leave. On some level, I could understand all the fear and confusion surrounding my decision. News organizations paint the world as a scary place with criminals and terrorists lurking around every corner. If it bleeds, it leads, right? Movies make you think you're going to be taken into sex slavery if you travel abroad. Every time my departure came up in conversation, my parents would express concern that I'd be kidnapped or end up on the nightly news another victim of a crime filled world.

Like so many others in America, they were convinced the world outside our borders was falling apart. Pictures of riots in foreign streets, threats against Americans, and general violence are some of the dominant images we see of the rest of the world. We are sent a fairly clear message, even if it is never spelled out directly: "The world is unsafe. Stay here."

Bombarded by this for decades, Americans, for the most part, think this myth is reality. They assume that citizens of other countries are uniformly hostile to us. "No one likes us out there," people, who had never been "there", would tell me. The myth of a fundamentally frightening world is only reinforced by a culture that doesn't put an emphasis on learning about the world. We don't study languages in school, history classes get cut or crammed into a year ("Here, let's learn the entire history of the world in eight months"), and we avoid overseas programs in college. The media doesn't focus on the world unless it relates to something bad, and our politicians don't seem to do much to encourage a more global view.

For most of our history, Americans' mental geography has been defined by the two oceans that separate us from the Old World. We've been taught to think of ourselves as secure and self-sufficient in our own hemisphere, a gigantic island unto ourselves. "Over there," generations of Americans were taught, meant decadence or sin or barbarism—or, at any rate, something very unwholesome.

Why would anyone travel overseas under these conditions? was the conventional wisdom. Need beaches? Head to Florida. The tropics? Hawaii. Desert? Arizona. Cold tundra? Alaska. Temperate forests? Washington. Americans simply don't see the need to go anywhere else when they can do it all in their own country. The result of all of this is that Americans may have a vacation culture, but we do not have a travel culture.

While I understood that on an intellectual level, butting against that headfirst was still an extremely deflating experience. To learn that the people whose approval I coveted most were so strongly against my plans took some of the wind out of my sails. When you crave the support of family and friends, and all they give you are reasons why you shouldn't do what you desperately want to do, it hurts. It's hard to stay strong when they dismiss your goals and dreams. And part of me thought that this was my fault—my fault for making a bad decision, or my fault for doing such a bad job of explaining how my life had gotten to the point where such a drastic decision seemed like the only way to find happiness.

So I kept the hurt inside. For the rest of the time leading up to my departure, my trip was like Lord Voldemort. It was "the thing that can't be named."

⊕

OVER THE YEARS, as blogging and social media have taken off, more and more people have started to travel the world and become semi-permanent nomads. Younger people, weaned on a diet of a global internet, travel more and to farther places. As the internet has allowed people to work remotely, and the term *digital nomad* entered our lexicon, it's less weird to quit your job to travel the world. To young kids today, it's more "Ohh, you're traveling like that blogger Nomadic Matt? Cool! I hope to do that too" than "You're crazy!" Even retirees are doing it more. I've seen a lot of "grey nomads" around the world. Long term travel isn't as crazy an idea as it used to be.

But, with no blogs or forums around in those halcyon pre-social media days of 2005 to cheer me on, I had to find the mental courage to do it myself.

I don't want to overstate the Americanness of the resistance I found when I announced my plans. Sure, people around the world who are lucky enough to live in travel cultures (New Zealand, Canada, Europe, and Australia come to mind) are encouraged to see more of the world, but they still have to overcome some basic human instincts that restrain us from walking out our front doors without looking back. For many of us, traveling takes a strong shove across the threshold. We need to be forced outside of our comfort zone. Fear of running out of money, fear of being alone, fear of possible danger, fear of leaving it all behind, fear of having no safety net—they're all universal worries. It's hard to just jump headfirst into the unknown and leave your entire life behind, with nothing but a backpack and a dream.

And that makes the hardest part of a journey the mental preparation. Once you are out of safe harbor, you feel the wind in your sails. Action begets action. As the shoreline drifts further away, the wind picks up and carries you like Gulliver to unknown lands. And once you're out there, your fears fade away as excitement and adventure takes over. You are too busy having fun to worry about worrying anymore.

But it can take a lot of work to get out of the harbor. Our comfort zones may make us unhappy at times, but more often than not, they keep us just happy enough to resist change. We may hate our routine, we may complain, we may daydream, but we don't change. It's the devil we know. It's where we are safe.

Society—and our DNA—tells us to favor safety over risk. Why leave the cave for where the monsters live when we can stay safe inside our shelter and live another day?

There is safety in the tribe. In routine. In your cave. To go out into the night is to court danger and death. Our primitive brain screams to us, *Stay here! This is safety! This is life!* So, while people everywhere dream of traveling the world, it is only those whose dreams are strong enough who get out and stay out on the road.

But strong enough for what?

Strong enough to overcome the fear of people who love you— people who, like my parents, still to this day email me travel warnings and news of terrorist attacks.

Strong enough to overcome the negativity of those who share your dream but not your intestinal fortitude. It's understandable to resent someone who lives your dream while, for whatever reason, you don't.

Strong enough to overcome the societal norms that tell you *not* to leave the safe harbor.

And, last but not least, your dream has to be strong enough to overcome your self-doubt. As I faced the daunting task of turning my dream into a reality, I asked myself the same hard questions I got from parents, coworkers, and friends.

Would I finish my MBA? How much money would I need? Where would I go? What would people say? Would I make friends? What credit card should I use? Were hostels safe? What the heck was travel insurance?

As I trudged through the seemingly endless preparations, I discovered a new daily mantra: "Fuck, what did I get myself into?"

I didn't so much care about my responsibilities. Bills disappear when you cancel the services that generate them. Cars go away when you sell them. And I knew my job at the hospital wasn't going to be my career so I had no worries about walking away from it.

What worried me was the personal skills I thought I needed to have to travel—the courage, the ability to go with the flow, the ability to talk to strangers, the confidence, the maturity—and whether or not I had enough of any of them after two two-week trips over two years to two countries that were full of English speaking travelers like me.

Yes, a lot of people travel the world. I saw hundreds of world travelers in Thailand. Unlike my Canadian heroes, I wasn't a hardened, experienced traveler. I was a sheltered child who never ventured far beyond his safe harbor. Did I really have what it took? Could I really fake a new me for so long? Would my secret nerdiness be outed? The fear and self-doubt I had whispered constantly in my ear.

All I could do each day was push the daily worry out of my mind. "I am not Magellan," I'd tell myself. I wasn't setting sail into the unknown. There were well-trod tourist trails. There were guidebooks that held all the instructions I needed, like a manual for assembling a dresses. I just had to follow their collective wisdom. If all those backpackers in Thailand could do it, why couldn't I? I made it in Costa Rica and Thailand. I made friends there. I talked to strangers. If eighteen-year-olds fresh out of high school can manage a year around the world, so could I.

And that's something I tell travelers now. We aren't Magellan. We aren't setting off into the blankness of history to chart new worlds. The next Magellans will colonize the moon. We're simply getting on an airplane and going where others have gone before. That's the difference between exploration and what we do—we're trying to have new experiences and learn about ourselves, not uncovering blank spots on a map. We're walking in others' footsteps, and we can be grateful to them even as we blaze new personal trails.

That doesn't make our journey less special. The world is full of new stories. New stories and adventures we would be a part of that would be special to us. I didn't need to discover Thailand to enjoy Thailand. The journey and experience was what mattered.

With thoughts like these, I quieted the self-doubting voice in my head. I put the disapproval of my parents and coworkers aside. I learned to accept all those negative voices, even if I didn't agree with them. If I was going to go away, I was going to have to do it on my own, because *I* wanted it for myself.

And I wanted it badly.

This trip was my chance to not only go on an adventure but finally shed the weight and insecurities of my past. This was my chance to go out there, live life, create stories, find opportunity, and become the me I've always thought I was in my head. To live out this character so much that I just became him.

I daydreamed the crazy things that would happen to me on the road. I'd make friends from around the world. I'd try adventure activities. I'd hike mountains and sail down exotic rivers. Locals would invite me out for drinks. I'd be sipping a latte, strike up a conversation with my beautiful waitress, and then the next thing I'd know we'd be at a wine bar, staring into each other's eyes. It was going to be just like those travel articles I'd read, or movies I saw and romanticized.

I knew there was a better world out there. I had seen it. I had felt its power to change me for the better.

Elsewhere was out there and it was calling me.

I was going to go, have the time of my life, come back in one piece with some stories to tell, and show everyone back home that travel is not a crazy idea.

I was going to prove them all wrong.

4

The Planning

The best laid schemes of mice and men often go awry.
—ROBERT BURNS

HERE'S ONE THING THAT IS CERTAIN about travel: All your plans will go out the window. Every budget you created, every hostel you researched, all the hours you spent researching will be meaningless the second you hit the tarmac as the reality of the road—the mishaps, the traffic-halting monsoons, the week-long rail workers strike—put kinks in your plans.

Yet, despite knowing all that, planning is still essential for long-term travel because it forces you to think clearly about your priorities—about what you value, what you want to do, where you want to go. If you want to go to four countries but had to cut one from your list, which would you cut? Do you want to travel in a bit more comfort, or stay on the road longer? How prepared are you to pare down your day-to-day life to save money for your trip? The specific answers you come up with don't matter all that much but the planning process helps you discover the kind of trip you want—and how much it's going to cost you.

Beyond that, planning travel is a rewarding experience in itself. Don't think of it as doing your homework—think of it as part of the adventure. It's fun, frustrating, exhilarating, and confusing all at once. There's nothing better than getting knee deep in guidebooks or lost on the web while researching your trip. It gives you ownership over your trip. It makes you an explorer before you've even set foot on foreign soil, as you discover places on paper that you'll see with your own eyes soon.

Planning can also help you stay positive and motivated when the opinions of your family and friends start to tip toward the judgmental and cynical.

Planning lets you stay focused.

Each decision you make brings you one step closer to departure. With each turn of a guidebook's page, your trip comes to life more and more. Planning helps you solve the jigsaw puzzle that is travel. How much will things costs? Where will you stay? How long will you stay in each place? What will you do? Who will you meet? What adventures will you get into? What sights will you see?

Planning, while rewarding, can also be hard work—figuring out what you value, in a disciplined way, always is. Would you rather carry clothes for all the seasons, or travel light? Do you withdraw foreign currencies before reaching your destination, even if you risk having your cash stolen or misplaced? Do you want to stick to packaged tours or guidebook routes, or do you want to go off the beaten path, even if that means exposing yourself to scammers? Can you stick to a budget? Can you save enough for a long trip, and what would you cut out of your day-to-day life to do so?

Those were some of the questions I sat down to answer as I outlined my first extended trip in 2006. I bought guidebooks to everywhere I wanted to go: Europe, Southeast Asia, Japan, Australia, and New Zealand. I piled them high on my bedroom floor, and I read them cover to cover, highlighting activities, costs, and potential routes.

Frugal by nature, I scoured the guidebooks for the cheapest versions of all the things I wanted to do, but as the days on my itinerary stacked up, so too did the amount of money I would need. If I was going to stay out on the road for an extended period of time, hopping from country to country, I was going to need lots and lots of money.

I created a detailed spreadsheet of how much money I had and all my current expenses. At this point in my life, I didn't even balance my checkbook. I couldn't tell you how much I was spending per month. It was something I had never done before.

But financial discipline is one of the keys to travel success. If you don't keep track of your expenses, you'll never make it to the finish line. You have a set amount of money that has to last the length of your trip. Budgets need to be followed.

That's why planning—even if your plans will go out the window—is so important. By setting your priorities, by researching costs, activities, hostels, buses, whatever, you can make your money last and stretch out to when that finish line will occur. You'll never be blindsided and you'll know yourself and your priorities.

Love eating out? Great! You're a foodie! Plan for it and eat away!

Suddenly finding yourself staying in hotels instead of hostels? That's a problem!

This is one of the things new travelers don't realize. When you have a set pool of money for your trip, money management is one of the most important aspects of travel.

You need to have the attention to detail of a CPA—before and while you're on the road.

I created a savings plan, put money into high interest CDs, and started creating budgets based on how much I knew I could save. I cut out things I felt were *wants* not *needs*. Things like going to movies, eating out, my daily Starbucks, and drinking out each weekend. They all fell under the "want" category and were the first to be cut out.

Next I worked on my "needs." I needed a place to live—but one that cost less. I moved out of my apartment and moved in with my parents to save on rent. (Plus meals from Mom were free, and I didn't have to cook them either, which meant more time to read travel forums and layout maps across my bed.) I needed to get to work—but in a way that cost less. I left my car in the driveway and took the bus everywhere.

I was mercenary in my cuts. There was nothing I wouldn't do to save one more penny for my trip. I added water to liquid soap containers to stretch it further. I ate peanut butter and jelly for lunch day after day, and then cut out the jelly.

My itinerary for this first trip was simple. I would begin in Prague then head down to Milan, through the Cinque Terre, over to Florence, Rome, and Naples, east to Corfu, then Meteora, Athens, the Greek islands, and finally onward to Southeast Asia. From there, it was on to Australia and New Zealand before heading home.

I had big dreams—dreams that were crushed the second I left home.

⊕

ONCE I GOT TO EUROPE, *all* my plans fell apart. Travel had other ideas for my carefully constructed agenda. In retrospect, I should have expected it, but at the time, any thrill I may have felt going off-script was tempered by disappointment (mostly in myself) of letting all my careful planning go to waste. In fact, none of that work went to waste—it shaped my sense of priorities and values for traveling—but that didn't change the fact that learning to let go of my plans was the most challenging part of this first big trip.

The first time I seriously scrapped my plans, I was in Rome. I had hit all of the Roman highlights—the Colosseum, the Sistine Chapel, lots and lots of gelato—and was ready for my next stop, which was supposed to be Naples. But every time I talked with a new friend in a hostel about travel in Italy, the city that came up was Venice, not Naples. They kept telling me that I had to see the canals and St. Mark's Square while I had the chance. Their descriptions were enthralling, but I still thought I had some pretty good things planned: I was going to gorge on pizza napoletana in the very birthplace of pizza, then I would tour the ruins at Pompeii, at which point I would be just a stone's throw from the island of Capri.

Then, as luck would have it, I learned that Ryanair—Europe's main budget airline—was having a €1 sale for direct flights from Rome to Venice. I took it as a sign. The CPA inside me took it as an opportunity to add money back into my budget after spending so much on drinks in Rome.

Before I knew it, I was getting lost in Castello, the city's main island. I strolled through the Piazza San Marco and gawked up at the ornate façade and domes of St. Mark's Basilica. I saw cafés where tourists drank overpriced wine, drank in small coffee bars where locals had their quick espresso, and wandered among the shops and eateries on Via Garibaldi. I passed down tiny streets, meandered over historic bridges that straddled the city's patchwork of canals, and found tiny, peaceful courtyards that acted as an oasis from the crowds.

At the hostel in Venice that night, looking up tomorrow's weather, reading the news, and checking my email, I saw a new message from an Austrian girl I had met during a road trip around the United States. Before I left for Europe, I had decided to drive across my own country for two months, hoping to learn about it before I learned about the world. Out near Sante Fe, I'd met Hannah in a hostel and she joined two other travelers I picked up for a few days. In her email, she suggested I visit her in Vienna. She would show me the sights. A free place to stay with a local? How could I say no? So I called a second audible, changed my plans again, and made the jump north over the eastern Alps.

Hannah and I visited the famed Schönbrunn Palace, built in 1600s as the summer home for the Hapsburgs. The palace was once situated in the countryside, where generations of monarchs hunted, fished, and escaped the heat of the city, but as Vienna has sprawled outward, it now sits in the suburbs. Though a major tourist attraction like the Schönbrunn is always mobbed by visitors snapping photos or listening to audio guides (something I do enjoy), I got lost in the little details that helped me block out the swarm of humanity and take me back to the palace's heyday—things like the thick red carpet and gold detailing on the walls of the Great Hall, or the water playing in the massive Neptune Fountain in the gardens outside. Those gardens, once the exclusive retreat of monarchs and nobles, are now free and open to the public, and we took full advantage. We climbed the garden's hill, cracked open a bottle of wine, and looked out over the city. The medieval spires of St. Stephen's church pierced the sky, dominating the landscape, and offering me a sense of calm that I'd made the right choice to come up to Austria, even if only for a day or two.

Amsterdam was my next stop. This, too, was unplanned. I found a cheap overnight train from Vienna and took it. My intricately planned itinerary was now officially torn to shreds. I was going with the wind now. In Amsterdam, I rented a bike and joined thousands of locals on a leisurely pedal around the old city's canals, taking in the features that have earned it the title of "the Venice of the north." At the Rijksmuseum, I came face to face with famous paintings—like Rembrandt's *The Night Watch*—that I thought I'd only ever see in books or on Wikipedia.

Next was Spain's Costa del Sol because I could stay with someone from my tour in Costa Rica. I sunned myself on white, sandy beaches, ate fresh calamari with crisp white wine, and discovered that I was quite fond of the Spanish habit of staying up talking and drinking until dawn, and then sleeping into the next afternoon.

In Athens, I climbed up to the Acropolis and gazed out at the tile roofs of the city stretching away in every direction. As a history lover, roaming the Greek ruins in town and visiting the museums was a dream come true. Somewhere in the past, my high school self was smiling. My CouchSurfing host, the first ever I had, showed me around with such warm hospitality that I still find myself constantly returning to Greece, pulled in by the nation's charms. I took a bus to Cape Sounion, and watched the sun set behind the ruined columns of the ancient Temple of Poseidon.

These are the memories that stick in my mind from the European part of my trip, and yet very few of these destinations were on my original itinerary. I started where I landed and I ended where I intended, but everything in between was a jumble of impromptu decisions, happenstance meetings, and lucky (price) breaks. This, I was realizing, was the whole purpose of planning your travels: to give you some key checkpoints that you can always rely on, and the flexibility to do whatever you want in between.

A plan is not a list of directions, it's a list of suggestions to take at your leisure. And that's okay, because the point of travel is to be flexible. If I left home in large part because I wanted out of the rat race of office life and middle-class predictability, I realized that there was no point in re-creating those attitudes on the road. To me, travel was supposed to mean freedom, and freedom meant the ability to change direction on a whim.

⊕

AS I REACHED Southeast Asia for the next leg of my voyage, I applied what I'd learned in Europe.

I went with the wind, where flights were cheap and friends had couches. When I didn't like a place, I packed my bag and left. When I loved a place, I stayed until I felt it was time to move on. In the end, my trip around the world looked nothing like the original itinerary I spent so long meticulously crafting.

Travel destroys plans with glee. In strange lands where you don't know how to navigate around, when buses don't show up and trains get delayed, when you get sick and can't find a doctor, travel is there to remind you that things can and will always go wrong. You'll find that the detailed plans you created—the timetables, itineraries, lists of things to do—melt away under the reality of the road.

The details are pointless. It is the shape of the journey you are creating for yourself that matters most. With each change in plans, I was learning to forget the little details and keep my eyes fixed on the big picture. Going to Venice rather than Naples was, in the scheme of things, inconsequential. Experiencing the freedom of going wherever I wanted, of relying on the wisdom of perfect strangers who would become fast friends— that was the big picture.

Just like a talented artist can draw a striking impression of a face with just a few lines, I learned to sketch my plans in less and less detail. "I'll just head east" or "I'll stay in France until Bastille Day." Anything more and travel will look at your plans and go, "That's not going to work for us!" and throw them out the window.

Learning to go with the flow is the most important part of travel planning. Travel is about letting things unfold and happen naturally. It's better to see fewer attractions and go deeper into a city or a region than to cast a wide net and go shallow. Going with the flow is how you get to know people and places better. It's how you avoid the stress and expense of constantly being on the move from place to place and attraction to attraction. That magical, romcom serendipity that people dream of on the road—that moment when a local befriends you or you stumble upon the most charming café or hole-in-the-wall restaurant—that stuff only happens when you let the day unfold without trying to assert your will against it.

That doesn't mean I've stopped planning. No. There's still joy in getting lost in blog posts, flight search websites, and guidebooks.

I spend countless hours researching where I'm going. That's still the part that makes the trip *real* and gives you something to look forward to. Even as I've become a travel expert, my love of overplanning has not gone away. But I've also come to enjoy throwing plans out the window even more and giving myself over to the moment.

We travelers are not alone in this weird relationship with planning and spontaneity. Film actors understand it, too. The best in the world will prepare for months for a role—losing weight, developing an accent, learning to box, researching history—and then on the day, when the cameras roll and the director yells action, they forget it all and give themselves entirely to the scene. It's scary to think about in the abstract, but in practice what an actor is doing is baking the spirit and the DNA of a character into their own bones so when it's time to perform, they *are* the character.

This is what we do when we plan. We absorb what is most important to us about travel and exploration as pursuits worthy unto themselves, so that when we land on terra incognita, and the bus is late or the hostel is full or the border is closed, we know what to do. The road is about learning to let go of all our plans, no matter how large or small, so we can grab hold of those serendipitous moments that turn into lifelong memories.

I embarked on this life so I wouldn't be tied down by plans and schedules. And even as my responsibilities have grown, I still hold onto this belief. If you want serendipity to happen, you cannot expect it come, and you cannot make it occur, but you must always be ready for it.

Almost every day, life gives me a little hint of where I need to go next—"Hey, try going that way!" And more and more,

I've learned to keep my ears open to that whispered hint, and to stop protesting, "But my plans!"

Because it is only when you submit to the world you hope to see that you can truly be present for the experiences you've so long dreamed about. Plans shouldn't be a security blanket—they should be a means to an end. And for me, that end has always been adventure.

5

The Start

To awaken quite alone in a strange town is one of the pleasantest sensations in the world.

—FREYA STARK

GROWING UP, I wanted to be an archeologist. My grandmother would give me books on unexplained phenomenon—the kind that talked about ancient aliens, Atlantis, and psychic encounters. Along with a steady diet of *Indiana Jones* movies, those books helped me craft an image of myself on wild adventures around the world. From my comfy, middle-class life, I dreamed about discovering something new and living the interesting life I read about or saw on TV.

Now, in 2006, on my first adventure in a foreign land without a tour guide or a friend to help shoulder the burden of navigating an unknown country, I was scared shitless. No amount of research and planning could quiet the world's oldest traveling companion, fear.

Almost immediately upon arrival in Prague, fear began to

whisper worries into my ear. Entering the busy arrivals area of Prague's international terminal, I looked around and saw signs in a language I didn't understand. This time there was no one to greet me. No driver to pick me up who already knew where I was headed. It was just me, and I had to figure out how the hell I was going to get to my hostel.

It was a simple enough task, but now that it was more than just a plan, fear arrived to resow the doubt of my friends and family into my fertile and frightened imagination. How was I going to do this alone?

"Where's the bus stop to town?" I asked at the exchange counter while exchanging dollars for Czech Koruna.

"It's outside to the right. Just follow the sign for the bus. There's a picture," the attendant said, as if I had asked the dumbest question in the history of the world.

Exiting the arrivals hall, I turned right and found my way to a bus stop. *This had to be it,* I thought. Why else would people be standing here with their luggage? I pulled out my guide and re-read the instructions on how to get into Prague until a bus finally came. I got in line. I told the driver where I wanted to go. He said something in Czech. Was that a question? Did he understand me? Unsure of what to do, I simply handed him the biggest note I had. He looked at me, gave me change, and waved me to the back of the bus.

"Train station, right?" I asked a little slower, in the way all Americans do when they are confronted by someone who doesn't speak English. As if, just by slowing down and enunciating the same words that were foreign to his ear, he would magically understand me.

He simply looked at me and waved me back again.

I took a seat near him, hoping being in his view would remind him I was a confused tourist, and he'd tell me when my stop arrived.

The last passengers boarded and the bus rumbled to life and set off. As we rolled through the countryside, I tuned out the chatter of the passengers and the roar of the bus and stared out the window, watching the countryside unfold in front of me. Outside were rolling green hills dotted with farms as little medieval towns and their church spires peaked up on the horizon. It was a rural, ancient land steeped in history. The sky was blue and the few white clouds scattered about made everything seem like a painting. This was the Europe I had imagined in my mind so many times.

I stared wide eyed and unblinking at this new and exotic place. This was it. *I was here.* I smiled and took an obscene amount of photos.

Slowly the countryside gave way to suburbs, which gave way to a bustling city center. As the bus stopped, the driver turned and pointed to a large building across the street.

"Train station. Metro," he said in heavily accented English.

From Prague's main station, I followed the directions I had printed out from the hostel's website. I took the subway to my stop, exited the metro and, for the first time, I took in Prague.

When the bus came into town, I was so worried about getting off at the right stop, I didn't really notice the city. I had imagined Prague as a city of beautiful cobblestone streets, medieval architecture, and ancient buildings. There would be tiny little squares and bustling cafés with waiters gliding among the tables serving wine to trendy Europeans.

But when I took in the scene outside the metro, my bubble burst. In front of me was a communist architect's wet dream. There were large ugly, grey rectangular apartment buildings with no outside décor except for the graffiti that now covered them. They were carbon copies of each other. There was a large ugly radio tower in front of me, the roads were paved with concrete not cobblestone, and there was trash everywhere.

As I searched for my hostel, the streets narrowed, graffiti proliferated, and the run-down buildings made me wonder who, if anyone, lived there. Fear crept back into my mind. Would I get mugged? Would drug addicts appear in doorways? Was this area going to be safe at night?

Eventually, I snaked through enough alleyways and turned enough corners to find my hostel in a small, dilapidated building with a nondescript sign hanging out front. Inside, there were a few computer terminals in the entranceway and a chatty Australian behind a desk.

I checked in and walked up an endless flight of creaky stairs. I had imagined European hostels as dirty, old, and cramped places with tiny showers covered in mold that looked as if they were last cleaned by the hippie backpackers who first founded the place. I wasn't far off.

My room smelled like the inside of a sneaker that someone only wore barefoot. In the summer. I cracked open a window to let in some air. The room was a square with six beds. Two bunk beds on one side and one (mine) on the other.

There were no lockers so I dropped my bag on the floor. As I sat on my lumpy bed, I smiled, and tried to put the shabbiness of the room into perspective.

I was *here*.

I made it.

⊕

AS AN INTROVERT, talking to strangers makes me nervous. I'd think of all the ways they might judge me and convince myself that, if we did talk, I'd stumble and stammer and wouldn't have anything interesting to say. Of course, I'd made friends on my previous travels before. But even then I was faking it. Deep down I was still the shy kid who could never fathom walking into a bar and walking out with a whole new group of friends. From time to time, I'd find ways to overcome my shyness—and then, when I least expected it, it would come crashing back.

My first night in the hostel was one of those nights. After a couple slices of pizza by myself at a place next door—I didn't know Czech food and day was turning to night by the time I checked in—I headed downstairs to the bar in hopes of meeting people.

As minutes passed like hours, I sat there alone watching the bar fill up with people interacting, laughing, smiling, and enjoying themselves. Too awkward to say anything, I used my jetlag as a self-justifying excuse for why I couldn't talk to anyone and went to bed early, hoping the next day would be a little better.

The next morning I wandered around Prague and found that my first impression was way off. Prague *was* a beautiful city. The city center had been wonderfully preserved. Like the location of many hostels in big international cities, it was just my neighborhood that was a rundown shithole.

I wandered Letenské sady, the gigantic park with an outdoor beer garden, where I stared out across the city from a lookout as couples posed for photos and an art student drew the skyline. I meandered through the nearby Královská zahrada, where the noise of the city fell away as the nearby St. Vitus Cathedral rose above the trees, and all that could be heard were the whispers of travelers talking about the park's beauty.

I crossed Charles Bridge, famous for the baroque statues of saints and heroes that line the sides. I later found out that all of the statues are replicas, and that the centuries-old originals had been placed in a museum for safekeeping. But at the time, I was just awed by the centuries of history on display. This was the city of Kafka and Kundera. Swept up in the excitement of it all, I made the mistake of paying one of the many artists on the bridge for some paintings of Prague, only to realize that I'd have to leave them behind in Europe: carrying them for a year was impractical, I didn't know anyone who could hold them for me, and mailing them home was more expensive than my budget could bear.

When you first start traveling solo, there's a sense of excitement about being alone. Unhindered by other people, you're the hero of your own story. You fantasize about all the people you'll meet and situations you'll get into as strangers take you under their wing and wonder with curiosity and excitement about your trip. There's no one to get in your way, no one to compromise with or negotiate with. There will be friends when you want them, but also solitude when you need it—a chance to unplug from other people and take time to think about what matters.

Just like well-laid plans, it's a romantic, reassuring idea that helps you get on the road but falls apart once it runs into real life. Few things push a person so completely and unceremoniously out of their comfort zone like solo travel. When you are with a tour group or friends, you can rely on someone else to do all the heavy lifting. Someone else can make the plans, talk to people, find the train station, navigate, keep track of money, or tend to you when you are sick. When you're solo, you have to do it all. You only have you. *You* have to figure out how to talk to people if you want to make friends. *You* have to figure out how to get to the airport, or your hostel, or how to find the right bus, or a good doctor. *You* have to figure out who is trustworthy or who is going to scam you. It's all on you—and that forces you to learn about people and places in a way you simply don't when you travel with others. Traveling solo, you learn who you are and what you are capable of. You learn how to be comfortable with only your own thoughts for companionship. In this sense, solo travel is a wonderful teacher, because it teaches self-reliance.

And that self-reliance is valuable even when you return from your travels. Self-reliant people know better than anyone what they can contribute to the world, what kind of life they want to lead, what kind of people they want in that life. Self-reliant people know that their confidence doesn't depend on the judgments of others. They know that they can make it anywhere—that they can be plopped down in the middle of nowhere and still figure it out. They know that they can face down their fear and anxiety. When I think of the self-reliance I learned on the road, I think of Ralph Waldo Emerson's famous words on the same topic. "Trust thyself:" he wrote, "every heart vibrates to that iron string. . . . Nothing can bring you peace but yourself." It's one thing to sense that those words have truth to them—it's another to try, as I tried, to live by them.

But, on the other hand, as richly rewarding as traveling alone can be, it has its costs and its downsides, as well. As you wander, eat, and sit in bars alone, you come to realize that traveling with no one but yourself for company can be its own kind of trial. Eventually the thrill of solitude wears off. Your mouth becomes dry from lack of use, and you forget how to have a good conversation. You turn to share experiences with someone only to realize there is no one there. Your aloneness has become loneliness.

Wanting human contact, I went back to the hostel bar on

my second night in Prague hoping I'd work up the courage to say something to someone.

The bar was dimly lit, with well-worn tables and sticky floors. On the walls were names and sayings from travelers long since departed. They had all come here looking for adventure. I wondered if they found it.

Like the night before, the bar filled up with travelers chatting together, talking like they were old friends, and I sat there in silence trying to find the right time and group to walk over to and say "Hey, mind if I join you?"

Fortunately, someone did the work for me.

"Hey! Want to join us?" said the short girl at the table next to me.

"Sure," I answered trying to hide my enthusiasm at the offer.

I moved over to their table. There were four of them and, when I sat down, they asked me the typical backpacker questions—where are you from? When did you get here? How long are you traveling for? Where are you going to next?

Boston. Today. About a year. Milan.

From the looks of us, the five of us could not have been more different. The girl who invited me over was a short, brown-haired, brown-eyed American girl who'd just come over from an under-the-table waitressing job in Greece after scaring away her traveling partner by peeing in their tent every time she got really drunk. Next to her was a tall, blond, thin-faced guy from Melbourne, Australia. Next to me was a bearded, bushy-haired, flannel-wearing chef from Oregon who, if he told me his name was L.L. Bean, I would have believed him. And then there was the quiet Canadian guy trying to travel for as long as he could make his money last. (One thing you learn with time is that every group you meet in a hostel has at least one Canadian.)

As we talked more, though, we discovered that we all shared a similar backstory. We were young, underemployed, and spending our summer in Europe seeing the sights, taking in the culture, and getting drunk before we went home and got real jobs. The only real difference between us was that they were all more experienced at hostel life than I was. I'd already encountered a few on my travels, but to that point I'd preferred cheap hotels and (even better) free lodging on friends' couches. But this—the crowded bar, the creaky stairs, the shared bathroom and musty bedroom with bunks—was the real hostel experience. Staying in uncomfortable places like this is a central part of the backpacking experience.

Centuries ago, young European nobles would take a Grand Tour through the Continent before settling down to their adult responsibilities back home. Now, with travel cheaper and more democratized thanks in large part to an international network of hostels, I looked around and realized we were all on our own modern, stripped down version of the Grand Tour.

Easy conversation and cheap beer spun the rest of our night into a blur. Stumbling upstairs much, much later in the evening, I entered my shared room, dizzy and triumphant. I'd done it. I had made friends. Everything was going to be all right. I was sure of it now.

⊕

A HOSTEL WITH FIFTY-CENT BEER, a crowd of twentysomethings, and precious little privacy means that a good night's sleep is never guaranteed. I entered my room to the sound of moans from a neighboring bunk. Was that . . . ? Yes, yes it was. I could sense movement on the bottom bunk, and made sure to clear my throat and shuffle my feet to announce my presence. But that didn't stop them. All I could do was put my pillow over my head and wait to pass out. Fortunately, the fifty-cent beer did its work, and in a few minutes I fell into a quick, drunk sleep, oblivious to whatever was happening in the other bunk.

Around dawn, as light began to shine through the thin curtains, the Kiwi girl staying in the bed across from me burst into the room with two guys. They clearly had a very wild night on the town. In epic disregard for others, they ripped the curtain down, letting the morning light pour in and waking everyone up.

"Shut up!" shouted the guy in the bottom bunk. He was American. I had seen him in the hostel but only briefly said hello to him. There was someone else still in his bed.

With lightning speed, the two guys turned around and asked if the girl in his bed was a dude.

The guy in bed quickly got out and, towering over the others, began to escalate the argument. "That was fucking rude," he said pushing one of the guys as the girl ran out of the room crying.

"Hey man! I'm just saying she didn't look too hot," one of the drunk guys said.

"Dude, I am going to clock you if you don't apologize."

The other drunk guy snickered.

"It's all good, mate," slurred the interloper.

"It's not fucking all good," Mr. America said stepping closer to him. "Apologize."

As a fight seemed imminent, the Kiwi girl stepped in.

"What he said was rude, but let's all calm down. We're super drunk. Let's just sleep," she said dragging her friend away from the red-faced American and into her bed.

The American grabbed his towel and walked out of the room. "Fucking assholes."

The other drunk guy, seemingly unsure what to do, went up into the empty bunk and passed out.

"Just relax. I have a flight in a few hours. Let's get some sleep," she said to her new bedmate.

As I tried to fall back asleep, I heard a noise from the bunk. Passing out as two people go at it in the next bunk under cover of darkness is one thing—but now I was trying to sleep as the Kiwi girl and her new friend started fooling around in full daylight, and I soon realized it was hopeless for me.

As the moaning grew louder, I knew there was no going back to sleep. I grabbed my towel and went to take a shower.

Fucking assholes was right.

By hostel standards, it wasn't an especially crazy night. I'm sure our hostel's owners and staff have had to break up dozens of drunken fights over the years, and launder more than their share of defiled bedsheets. And I'm sure hostel owners all over Prague, and all over Europe, could share similar stories. It's not that their establishments attract an especially rough crowd—it's that traveling without strings attached turns hostels into reflections of that unbounded freedom.

A hostel like mine in Prague is full of young people experiencing freedom from obligations and responsibilities for the first time. Of course they're liable to get a little carried away with the excitement. When a bunch of kids want to get their ya-ya's out, a hostel is where they put them. But more to the point, it's the transitory nature of nomadic life that makes hostels the occasionally out-of-control places they can become. You don't rip curtains open and wake up a room full of sleeping people if you have to deal with them the next day, and the day after that. You don't have sex while your roommate is trying to sleep in the next bed if you're going to be roommates for more than a night.

The promise that we're going to interact with the people in our lives day after day keeps us civil—we don't break the rules today, even if we want to, because we know we're going to have to deal with the consequences tomorrow. But on the road, there's no guarantee you'll see that person tomorrow (or ever again), so the only thing keeping you civil is whatever self-restraint you happen to internalize. I love the freedom of travel, but I also realize that, while it can bring out the best in us—our sense of adventurousness, curiosity, and creativity—it can also sometimes bring out the worst.

Despite all that, I still came to love hostel life. That transitory quality helped me feel like a new me every time I checked into a new place. No one knew who I was until I stepped into that common room or bar. I could always fake it until I made it. I could be anyone I wanted to be—and so could everyone else. I could be a party guy on Monday, an introvert on Tuesday, a stoner on Wednesday, a loudmouth on Thursday, a jokester on Friday. I could cultivate any one of these selves on any given day.

The trick is learning how to value hostels for what they are—cheap lodging, a ready supply of new friends for the road, and a ready supply of fresh chances—without getting sucked into the same pattern of drinking, hooking up, and passing out night after night. That's just another kind of routine—and I went on the road to get away from routines.

And if I screwed up—if I made a joke that didn't land, or found myself alone at a table while everyone else hit it off—tomorrow was always a new day with a new set of people. Every day was a fresh start, a second chance to be that kind of ideal self—confident, secure, inwardly happy—I always wanted to be.

Of course, travel doesn't let you escape your past. Your demons will always find some space in the bottom of your backpack. But travel does give you multiple fresh starts to deal with them, multiple ways of experimenting with the new self you want to become.

⊕

EXCEPT FOR A BRIEF MEETING with my new Australian surfer friend a few years later, I never saw those travelers from Prague again.

Yet, for a moment, we were the best of friends. They gave me hope that I would be all right. Sitting at the hostel, I fretted about being able to make friends. I was scared to talk to people. Yet here I was two days later, hugging people who were just recently strangers, feeling like I was leaving my best friends behind.

All those fears I had when I landed in Prague—the worries about being lost, not making friends, and ending up alone—melted away as I got on the plane to Italy. The seeds of doubt that my insecurities, family, and friends had planted in my mind had proved false, or at the very least remained dormant.

I felt like I aged a million years in Prague. I came to the city with equal parts delusions of grandeur and fear that my parents and coworkers would be right, but we were both wrong.

It turns out that everyone else in the hostel is just someone trying to see some of the world and find a friend along the way. They hold the same fears and seek the same joys as you. They, too, are looking for someone to say, "Hey, want to join us?"

Hostel life forces you to confront the years of conditioning so many of us have endured about what we "need" from our lives: fineries, nicer stuff, better shoes, bigger TVs. Hostels can teach us just how little we need to be really happy.

When you're in a hostel in the middle of nowhere, and

you're sitting on a couch that can barely hold itself together, and you're drinking cheap wine, and only really picking up every other word of a conversation—when you do all that and you're happy!—you realize how much artifice and nonsense gets accumulated in your brain.

You begin to realize that everything is going to be all right. That the world isn't the scary place people told you it would be and that danger doesn't lurk around every corner. That there are wonderful people out these. People with the same wants as you.

And that some of them are going to have a profound impact on your life—whether you're ready for it or not.

6

Finding Your Kindred Spirits

I have found out that there ain't no surer way to find out whether you like people or hate them than to travel with them.

—MARK TWAIN

I LIKE TO GROUP PEOPLE into two camps: those who have stayed in a hostel and those who have not. For me, it's as revealing as knowing where you grew up or what your favorite movie is, because it reveals a lot about your character.

There you are. You enter your hostel or guesthouse, strike up a conversation with another traveler, and just like that you're best friends. You hang out, eat, drink and sightsee together for days.

For that time and place, you two (or three or four) do everything together and joke as if you had been friends forever. You're besties.

There is no past or future. Nothing about who you were back home, how old you are, what you do for work, your last relationship, or where you're from matters. You accept each other for who you are right there because that's all you have.

But then, as quickly as it started, it's over. You go one way and they go another.

Vague promises of meeting up and staying in touch fade away as you get further and further from the moments you spent together. Emails and messages begin to slow to a trickle. There's no ill will, no fight that splits you up—just the sobering truth that in a specific time and place, you made a connection, but now that time and place are gone and so are they. You were strangers in a strange land and, with necessity being the mother of all invention, you gravitated toward each like celestial objects caught in each other's orbit for no other reason than that you both existed.

As a backpacker, you get good at saying good-bye.

Prague was the first place where I had one-city friends. I met five amazing people there and, when it was all over, they were gone. Off to various parts of the world on their own adventures.

During my next stop in Florence, I struck up a conversation with a Canadian named Peter at our hostel. He was WWOOF-ing (Worldwide Opportunities on Organic Farms) around Europe, working in exchange for free room and board, in hopes of learning about food so he could be a cook. Tall, with long hair past his shoulders, glasses, and a goofy expression welded to his face, he, too, was traveling solo.

We spent five solid days sightseeing, taking day trips through the surrounding area, and partying our nights away. He was my best friend in Florence. Nay, for that time and place, he was my *only* best friend.

But, when it was time to move on, he too was gone.

"See ya later!" we said.

At the time, I thought we really would. I was new to the road.

You don't make connections like this every day! We were besties now. *Of course*, we would see each other again.

But life got in the way as it always does. People move on, settle
down, get jobs, find new friends, get married, and have kids.

It's a cycle that repeats itself a thousand times on the road
with everyone you meet.

From the folks in Prague to the couple I met in Panama to
the people on my tour around New Zealand, to the CouchSurfing hosts in Europe, to Dutch guys I camped with in Australia,
to those really freaking awesome folks I road-tripped in the
United States with, the two guys I backpacked Thailand with,
my friends from Ios, Bulgaria, and to the thousands of other
people I've shared magical moments with over the decade, life
simply got in the way.

For a time, we were each other's best of friends, partners in
crime, and sometime lovers.

Yet, as we all wander further along life's path, they begin to
fade in our memories. Their names get buried deep down the
text message queue on our phones. Every once in a while they
will pop to the forefront of our mind, usually because of something we just encountered reminds us of them, and we wonder
with a sense of longing:

What are they doing? Do they still travel? Did they make it
all the way around the world like they hoped? Are they happy?
Married? Do they like their jobs? Are they healthy? Are they
even alive?

There's no bad blood or animosity. Just the truth that they
were in your life for that moment and then their part in the play
of your life was over and it was time for new characters to
appear.

It was a truth I learned to deal with. Our paths may not

intersect again but my friends' effect on my life will remain with me forever. They taught me to let go, laugh, love, be more adventurous, push myself, and so much more.

This all sounds incredibly romantic and tragic, I know, and probably also fantastical to someone who has never had the privilege of these intense experiences. But this happens all the time to people whose interactions are compressed by time and space. The same thing happens at summer camps, for instance. You come from an entirely different world than the kids assigned by chance to your cabin, and barely a week later you're brothers from another mother, sisters from another mister.

Travel compresses relationships.

In its fiery forge, travel strips away the outside world and, with nothing but the now, amplifies the intensity of all your experiences. With no past or future, you get to know people as they are in that moment. We may ask basic, vague questions about the past when we meet each other initially, but it's really just a different way to talk about the weather. It's a placeholder until we figure out what else to say, to get us closer to what we really want to know: do you want to go sightsee, get a drink, or head to the beach? With the unspoken understanding that you have limited time together, you focus on the here and now.

But, sometimes, you meet people who will be more than just a temporary friend for a day. Sometimes, when travel filters out the noise, you form deep and powerful bonds with people that no time or distance can pull apart.

⊕

THE FIRST TIME THIS MAGIC happened to me was in Thailand at the end of 2006. While emailing my parents to let them know I was okay, I saw a message in my inbox:

"Matt, I'm stuck in this placed called Ko Lipe. I'm not going to meet you as planned, but you should come down here. It's paradise! I've been here a week already. Find me at Monkey Bar on Sunset Beach.—Alice"

I was on the island of Ko Phi Phi, in between the mainland and Phuket. Alice, a friend from myspace, was supposed to meet me in Krabi, a tourist destination famed for its limestone karsts, rock climbing, and kayaking. I had never met her before. We had found each other in a group for travelers. In those long ago days, Southeast Asia didn't have hostels. You had cheap guesthouses. I was worried that without the forced connection of a hostel dorm, I wouldn't meet anyone. I'd be alone again. Seeing our itineraries overlapped, I messaged Alice to meet up. *At least, I'll have one friend if all else failed,* I thought.

I looked up Ko Lipe. There was only a small mention in my guidebook. It was really out of the way and would require a solid day of travel to get to. But, as I looked around the bustling internet café and out onto the busy street, it was clear that this place was not the tropical island paradise I had come to know Thailand as. It was crowded, the beach was filled with dead coral, boats seemed to ring the island, and the water was polluted with a thin film of . . . well, I didn't want to know. A quieter, calmer paradise held great appeal.

Two days later, I took the ferry to the mainland, a long bus to the port city of Pak Bara, and then the ferry to Ko Lipe, where I wandered to the top deck to find a guy playing a guitar. His name was John. He was meandering around Asia with his girlfriend, Sophia, until they were ready to move to New Zealand, where they planned to work, buy a house, and eventually get married.

"Where are you guys staying?" I asked as we lounged on the deck.

"We found a resort on the far end of the island. It's supposed to be cheap. You?"

"Not sure. I'm supposed to stay with my friend, but I haven't heard back yet. I'll figure it out when I get there."

The ferry neared the island and came to a stop. There was no dock on Ko Lipe. Years before, a developer tried to build one, but the project was canceled after protests from the local fishermen who could see the end of their lucrative business shuttling tourists from the ferry to the shore if this dock came to pass. Then the developer mysteriously disappeared and that was the end of that.

John, Sophia, and I went to their hotel, joined by Pat, an older Scottish guy, who was also looking for a place to stay. The hotel overlooked a little reef and the small Sunrise Beach, which would become our main hangout spot during our time on the island.

As we walked to the other side of the island to Sunset Beach, where Monkey Bar and Alice were located, it became clear very quickly that she was right: Ko Lipe *was* paradise. Lush jungles, deserted beaches, warm, crystal-clear blue water, and friendly locals. Electricity was only available for a few hours at night, there were few hotels or tourists, and the streets were simple dirt paths. This was the place I had been looking for since the islands around Thailand jumped out of the pages of my guidebook.

We found Alice quickly. Sunset Beach was not big, and Monkey Bar, a small thatch-covered shack with a cooler for drinks and a few chairs, was the only bar on the beach.

After a few days, I moved into a bungalow in the middle of the island. Nestled behind a restaurant that served the best squid around, this hardwood structure painted red, with a white roof, small porch, and near-barren interior—a bed, a fan, and mosquito net—seemed to be built by the family for a wave of tourism that had yet to come.

Our days were spent playing backgammon, reading, and swimming. We rotated beaches, though we mostly hung out at the beach by John and Sophia's. Within swimming distance was a rock outcrop with a sheer drop that provided excellent snorkeling. We'd occasionally leave Ko Lipe to fish, dive, and explore the deserted islands in the nearby national park. At night, we'd eat and drink at Monkey Bar with Alice, Pat, a German couple, Bill, the British bartender who was there all season, a few locals, and whoever else joined our motley crew, until the power went out.

There wasn't much to do, but in simplicity we found joy.

The days passed by endlessly.

"I'll leave tomorrow" became my mantra.

It was great to get the chance to hang out with Alice, but it was John, Sophia, and I who formed a mini-group within the group.

"What are you guys going to do when you get to New Zealand?" I asked them one night over drinks and under the fading incandescent lights of the Monkey Bar.

"We're going to work for a few years and build a life there. We have nothing that's pulling us back to England," said John.

"I'm going there on this trip so I'll visit. It's my last stop on the way home," I replied.

"You can stay with us. Wherever we are," said Sophia as she passed a joint to me. (Another thing we did to pass the time.)

It was only when Christmas decorations appeared on storefronts and families flooded the beach—like magic they all appeared in a single day—that we became aware of time again.

Christmas meant I would have to leave soon. My visa was only valid until just before New Year's. I'd have to head to the nearby Malaysian border to renew it so I could have more time in the country and keep traveling. There was no way to extend it from where I was.

John, Sophia, and I decided to have our own Christmas together. We wore our best clean shirts and wandered over to Coco's for its luxury Western Christmas dinner.

"I got you guys a gift," I said as I handed Sophia a necklace I saw her eyeing a few days before and John a ring he had admired.

They were deeply touched, and is so often the case with great, new friends out on the road, they had the same idea.

"We got you something, too," John said.

It was a hand-carved necklace with a Maori fishhook on it, the symbol of the traveler.

I loved it.

After I left, I ran into John and Sophia a few weeks later walking down Bangkok's Khao San Road. Shocked at such a random event, we hugged, talked about where we had been and what we had seen, and spent the next few days picking up like we had never left Lipe.

Years later, when I finally went to New Zealand, I spent Christmas and New Year's at their home in Auckland. I had never made it on my original trip around the world but when I made it, they were the first people I wanted to see. They were working jobs—and I was still a traveler. Life had moved on for both of us. We had new friends and lives but we still laughed at the same jokes, had the same sense of humor, and got on like we had known each other for several lifetimes. Everything else that had happened in between melted away and we were back on that beach talking about things only travelers discuss when there are no other cares in the world.

⊕

IN THE TINY TOWN of Buñol, Spain, tens of thousands of people gather every year for the famous La Tomatina festival, the largest tomato fight in the world.

La Tomatina has its roots in the carnivals and harvest festivals that have enlivened European towns for centuries, but this particular festival started in 1945. A parade was scheduled in Buñol that day, and one of the participants got so angry when his giant costume head fell off that he trashed a tomato stand and sparked a huge food fight. The next year, on the same day, kids came back with a stash of tomatoes and reenacted the food fight, and it's been a Spanish tradition ever since. It hasn't always been observed, though: For several years, it was banned, and would-be food fighters were even arrested for tomato possession. In 1957, they held a satirical protest of the ban, putting a giant tomato in a coffin and burying it to the sound of funeral marches. Ultimately, the government relented, and La Tomatina has been a tradition ever since.

When I think of all that history, so rooted in the experiences, stories, and food of one particular place, it's hard not to feel like an outsider when you go. In 1945, I imagine, the thrill of a wild, spontaneous food fight must have been tied up with the joy of World War II having ended that very summer. In the 1950s, protesting the tomato ban must have been a covert way of protesting Spain's Fascist government. You don't have to know any of that history to show up in Buñol, buy your ticket, and pick up a tomato, of course. The town welcomes the tourist money, but seeing a local tradition turned into a global fixture must be the source of some complicated emotions. It certainly was for me. Would I be turning a special tradition into kitsch by partaking? Was I not taking La Tomatina seriously enough? How does one even take a tomato food fight seriously in the first place?

The year I went to La Tomatina, I stayed in a six-bed dorm room with a Alex, a Malaysian man from Paris, Jessie and Joel, twins from Portland, and Claire and Nick, two Australians backpacking around Europe.

The day of the event we took a train into Buñol and jostled through the crowds until we made our way to the town square. The crowds got thicker as the streets grew narrower. Eventually, we found a plaza to stand in and took position in the back. People climbed up ledges, trees, and positioned themselves from roofs. Everyone searched for the high ground.

The bell rang and the mayhem started. Big garbage trucks overflowing with tomatoes rolled through the town. Soon everyone was covered in red, tomatoes smacked off your head, and the rivers ran deep with tomato juice. Being in the back is not a prime tomato-picking position, but I did my best to pick up half smooshed tomatoes slick with juice and let fly at anyone nearby. I was having so much fun, laughing and shouting through it all, that I often got tomatoes in my mouth. Above us, a Japanese tourist had climbed a doorway for a better vantage point only to get pegged with dozens of incoming red missiles that knocked him off the edge into the crowd below.

And then, as quick it started, it was over. The one-hour festival felt like it went by in thirty seconds. As the last of the tomatoes splatted to the ground, we all lined up to be hosed down by fire trucks. I've heard that Buñol's main square is especially shiny, because the acid from the tomatoes has polished it over the years.

Over the next few days, our group explored Valencia. We were bonded by our shared experience and spent all waking hours together. In them, I found compatriots. It was as if we had known each other our whole lives and the universe conspired to bring us together for this festival so we could realize we had been friends forever—we just didn't know it yet.

Two weeks after La Tomatina, Claire, Nick, and I were in Barcelona together. Alex had returned to Paris and the twins, after spending a day with us had, to continue on to Venice. As the remnants of our group walked down Barcelona's Barri Gòtic, joking around and busting each other's chops, our new friend Michelle could sense our closeness.

"Did you guys go to school together? I think it's pretty cool that three people from different places have been friends for so long."

"Actually, we've only known each other for two weeks," Nick said.

"Wow! Really?" a shocked Michelle said. "You have so many inside jokes and act like you've been friends forever."

To be fair, two weeks together is a lifetime in backpacker time. But even so, we acted like we had known each other since childhood because in many ways we had. We didn't have the adult world to get in the way of our friendships. We just had playtime. And, like kids at playtime, we found the childlike sense of friendship that knows only joy, not judgment.

Because the other thing travel helps you do is confront your judgments and perception of people.

People like Dave and Matt.

⊕

DAVE, ALONG WITH his close friend Matt, were two Canadian oil workers I met in Thailand during the Full Moon Party.

Now, months later, they were hosting me in Perth for a few days. As travelers, we are always saying good-bye and promising to let someone crash on our couch when they are in our city. Sometimes these promises become a reality.

When I posted on Facebook that I was heading to Australia, Dave offered up his couch and I accepted. But, as I looked at these two surfer dude oil workers sitting up front in the car on the way to their place from the airport, I wondered if we'd still get along. When you live in the travel bubble, getting along is easy. There's just the fun you are having right now. You can be whoever you want to be and if some people don't like it, you know they are probably leaving soon anyways.

The real world is different. You have bills to pay. Responsibilities. Jobs. Commutes. Things to worry about. You aren't on the move anymore, rather you are now firmly planted in one place, building a life.

What were these guys like back home? Were they clean? Messy? Drinkers? OCD? Early risers? Politically opposite? Do they read books? Does the day to day of being at home make them irritated? Actually, *why* did they move to Perth? As I began to wonder about these questions, I realized I didn't *really* know anything about them. When you travel, you don't ask these kinds of questions. For all I knew, they could be members of a cult.

Fortunately, my fears of personality clashes were unfounded. Dave and Matt proved to be gracious hosts, taking me to the beaches, local bars, restaurants, showing me Australian movies so I'd be able to know pop culture as I traveled the country. It was as if we had never left that beach in Thailand. I actually think it was that Thailand beach mentality that never left them. They brought it home with them in their carry-on, from the duty free shop that is the nomadic experience.

At home, we judge people right away. By their dress, their

phone, their style, their posture. We see the Goth going down the street and think "weirdo." We see kids skating in parks and think "punk." We see white guys in dreads and think "hippy." We gravitate to people like us and rarely venture outside our homogenous social circle.

But, when you are on the road, you hang with all types of people. Your desire to make friends trumps everything. You don't know people's history or past. You don't know what "group" people fall into. You don't care because it doesn't matter. A friend is a friend.

That forces you to expand your mind, tear down your barriers, and toss out your judgments, which is how I ended up bonding with two tatted surfers so much that I ended up at their weddings.

Because I didn't judge them when I met them. I didn't bring my prejudices with me to Thailand. I accepted them for the nice people they are. The real world clutters our mind with prejudices and stereotypes so much that it keeps you from enjoying the rich relationships that a variety of people can bring.

Travel is an antidote to that.

Travel friendships are snapshots in time. When you meet up again, it's as if you are being transported back to those moments. You're again carefree children exploring the world. Life hasn't got in the way for you.

Time has stood still. You lived two separate lives—and none of the drama or problems from those lives bleeds into your friendship. You reminisce, drink some beers, and laugh at the same dumb jokes. It's never awkward.

That's why I put people into two groups. Those who have spent their days in hostels, forced to turn strangers into friends, and confront their prejudices tend to be more open minded, relaxed, and friendly. We're used to being alone. To not have a support system. To have to take a deep breath and ask that group of ten if that seat is free.

We're ok with a wide range of people. We learned that people are people and to never judge a book by the cover. We've learned that it doesn't matter what "group" you fall into. All that matters is how you act.

Travel creates opportunities to meet people you wouldn't give a second thought to walking down the street. It strips away the artifice and lets you walk away with some of the best friends you'll ever have—friends who will be there your whole life, ready to pick up right where you left off whenever you happen to meet up again.

7

Life as an Expat

Travel does what good novelists also do to the life of everyday, placing it like a picture in a frame or a gem in its setting, so that the intrinsic qualities are made more clear. Travel does this with the very stuff that everyday life is made of, giving to it the sharp contour and meaning of art.

—FREYA STARK

SO THERE I WAS, late at night, with my backpack next to me, sipping ouzo in a little taverna near the Acropolis in Athens, when the bartender—a kind older gentleman with salt-and-pepper hair and a thick mustache—stopped polishing the bar, put his towel over his arm, and approached my table.

"My friend," he said, "it looks as if you are new in town and haven't found a place to stay. I am just closing up, and my family is celebrating the christening of my brother's newborn son. It would be an honor to invite you to join us."

How could I say no? I hopped on the back of his motorcycle, and in a short while I was in his brother's garden courtyard, watching the family roast a whole goat and sing and dance into the night. I was a new member of the family. They were kind enough to offer me a guestroom. A night turned into three and they became my hosts, showing me around the city, and teaching me some useful Greek phrases. In the morning, his brother's wife always had breakfast prepared for me. At night, we drank ouzo while I learned (poorly) how to make Greek food.

When I left a few days later, I promised to keep in touch and send postcards from my future travels.

It was one of those serendipitous travel experiences you always hope for. It was right out of a book—and there I was living it.

Except I wasn't. Life isn't really like that.

That story never happened.

There are lots of magical moments when you're on the road, but ones like this—where you fit seamlessly into local life, where you get invited to parties and home-cooked meals and quirky adventures, where you eat pray love—are as rare as winning the lottery.

That is not to say that lightning does not strike every once in a while. These serendipitous moments *have* happened to me. The random students in Munich who invited me to a rock show; the couple at the restaurant in Galway who took my friend and me out for after-dinner drinks; the bartender in Cambodia who invited us to her home in the countryside; the Danish family who took me to their Sunday dinner.

These things do happen, but they are rare, because real-life travel is not that romantic, or that easy.

On the road, there are countless little casual encounters with locals and travelers. But it's one thing to meet people at bars, in restaurants, or on some local bus. To chat about where you're from and what brought you here, to share a few laughs, to sightsee, or talk while on a tour.

And it's something else entirely to get invited into someone's home and into their daily life. To get off the bus and have someone go "Wait. Why don't you join my family for dinner tonight?" To have the waitress say, "Stay after closing and have some drinks with us." To go from the bar to someone's backyard BBQ, friend's house party, third cousin's wedding, or be the plus-one in someone's road trip. To feel as if you've gone from a stranger to a guest—to someone who actually belongs.

Most people don't want to make friends with folks who are about to leave, and travelers are *really* good at leaving. Locals don't want their daily lives interrupted so casually. Heck, you probably wouldn't either. We have things to do. We want to make friends with people who will put down roots. People we can count on. So, to really enter someone's private world, to have those deeps moments become common place and to really get to know a place, you have to flip the script and do that one thing that traveler's aren't good at: staying put.

⊕

STEPPING OUT OF THE LARGE nineteenth-century redbrick train station after my overnight train ride from Vienna into a melee of trams, bikes, and old brick buildings, I gazed out over a patchwork of canals and tiny cobblestone streets. To my left was the Basilica of St. Nicholas, a beautiful baroque church that would become my favorite. In front of me, a mass of people were trying to get to and from work. Making my way through the chaos, I followed the directions on my map toward my hostel, located in Amsterdam's sex-and-beer-filled red light district.

I spent my first days in the city like most backpackers: high as a kite. Coming from the United States, the openness to smoking everywhere was a novelty I couldn't get enough of. Neither could any of the other backpackers. The city had a reputation with travelers for vice. Amsterdam was the city you partied in as you traveled across the Continent on your backpacking trip. It was the place where, at least for many of the Americans I met on the road, you first started to feel yourself shedding some of that puritanical American-ness.

Still, after a few days, I became bored. It was 2006 and I was five months into my trip around the world. Was this what travel was all about? In other cities, you partied and visited the sights. Here, you just seemed to party until you couldn't see straight. I liked to smoke but that wasn't the only thing I had come here to do. It was a sharp contrast to Vienna, where I got to see the city from a local's point of view. That was the kind of travel I wanted. I didn't want to just sit around and smoke weed *all* the time. There was a huge city out there. A beautiful, historic city filled with people and sights and art and history that I wanted to get to know. After all, Amsterdam didn't become famous, so many centuries ago, as the number one place in Europe to blaze up and lose your mind. It became famous as the trading and financial hub of a continent, as a place of free thought and free religion, at a time when other European nations were still executing heretics. It was the home of the stately canal-side mansions of great merchant princes, the inspiration for Rembrandt and all the other great Dutch master painters. Weed is such a late, and minor, addition to all that makes Amsterdam special. Yet people to this day—despite open access to recreational marijuana around the country—still cross the Atlantic to get it in the Netherlands and miss what actually matters.

A week into my visit, I found myself wandering the city, on one of those night walks that leads you to places that either leave indelible marks on your memory or feel fuzzy years later, like you may have imagined them. I wanted something more than just another coffee shop. On this walk, I found myself standing in front of the city's casino. Though I was on a traveler's budget, playing some poker appealed to me more than getting high. After graduating college, my friends and I started a weekly poker game and became hooked on the game. I loved the psychology of reading people and played poker to fund some of my trip.

I sat down at a full table of locals playing 2-5 No-Limit. I was on the end and, when I finally decided to join a hand, the dealer said something to me in Dutch. "I'm sorry, can you repeat that in English," I meekly said, embarrassed that I had used the most tourist of expressions.

I had outed myself as a foreigner, which is always a dicey gamble when you're outside the tourist zones. Fortunately, it turned out to be a good thing because it gave the locals something to ask me about: how I ended up at the poker table and not in the coffee shops where the other tourists seemed to go.

I told them the truth: I was curious about life in Amsterdam, and smoking endless amounts of pot had lost its luster for me. They appreciated my curiosity and we talked through the night.

The two nearest to me and I bonded the most. There was Greg, who was older, tall, of African descent, with bright smile, warm laugh, and, to my advantage, shitty at poker. The other was Marteen, young, tall (like most Dutch men), bald, slightly brooding, drank like a fish, and smoked like chimney.

I had so much fun listening to their stories I went back to the casino the next few nights, because I knew they would be there. Along with the other players at our table, they made me feel like I was part of something more. I wasn't just a backpacker getting high in hostel bars and walking around taking pictures of museums. I was a *traveler* getting under the skin of the place and getting to know the people who lived there. I was endeavoring to understand the culture and the players were my guides the way Hannah had been in Vienna.

They told me about life in the city and restaurants and bars to visit that tourists didn't know about. Poker was our bond and, for those brief hours we were together each night, I felt like I, too, was a local.

I had left to travel the world in order to learn about it, and as much as I loved seeing museums, taking walking tours, and having short conversations with the people I crossed paths with, none of that really gave me a deep understanding of the places I visited. I felt like I had learned more about Amsterdam in those few nights than I had for all of the first week I'd been in the city. And I don't think I would have learned half of it had the guys at my poker table looked at me as some kind of rubbernecker or interloper or worst, a pest.

As a traveler, this is something you always need to be mindful of. If you fall into the tourist traps, or even follow the well-worn paths of hostel-living backpackers, you can appear to the local population kind of like locusts. You arrive seasonally in a swarm, create long lines and overtake once quiet streets, and when you leave everything is a mess and you've left nothing positive behind (besides tourist dollars) from your visit. You've only consumed. You've only taken from them. When you stay awhile, you balance those scales. Your relationship with the locals becomes more symbiotic, and you even have a chance to make a few honest-to-goodness friends.

As the days passed, I kept delaying my departure from Amsterdam. I had found local friends. Friends I didn't need to say good-bye to after a few nights. These folks were staying around and, for the second time in my trip, I felt like a traveler. Someone who was doing more than scratching the surface of a place behind my camera but getting to know a place deeper and learning how the world and its people worked.

They showed me Oosterpark, on the eastern side of the city. It was a small quiet square park, lined with willow trees and small ponds with ducks, where seniors sat around feeding the birds. It was a place locals like because they could avoid all the tourists and stoners who litter Vondelpark.

They introduced me to bitterballen, the bite-sized, deep fried Dutch meatball snack that looks like falafel on the outside but tastes like Sunday pot roast on the inside.

Weeks passed. I fell into a routine. I learned basic Dutch phrases from the other players at the casino, slept late, and used my winnings to finance an endless supply of nice meals, museum trips, and cannabis. I walked for hours upon hours reaching the city's fringes, trying to get lost in the canals and tiny streets that make Amsterdam so famous. The kind of thing you might do when, in the back of your head, you keep saying "I could live here," and you suddenly find yourself comparing all the neighborhoods.

But all good things come to an end, including my European visa, and it was soon time to head to Southeast Asia. After close to two months in Amsterdam, I couldn't stay in Europe any longer.

On my last night in Amsterdam, my new friends and I went out for dinner, played some poker, and went for a final round of drinks. I told them where I was headed and how much longer I planned to be on the road. We reminisced—something you can't really do when you don't spend more than a couple days in one place, or with one group of people. They appreciated that *I* appreciated the fact that Amsterdam is more than the red light district and tulips and windmills and coffee shops. That's all tourists and backpackers think of when they come to Amsterdam, they said. Though, by their own admission, they were only guessing. They'd never actually met a backpacker, let alone had conversations with one. And why would they have? Backpackers never strayed this far off the beaten path. And how many tourists do you go out of the way to meet in your home? None, right? There's no reason to do so.

If there were merit badges given out for nomads, I felt like I would have earned one for being the first traveler these guys ever talked to and got to know. When we parted ways at the end of the night, they invited me down to Utrecht on my next trip through the Continent. Amsterdam is great, they said, but it's not the real Netherlands. There is so much more to the country.

As a person, you know that intellectually. All it takes is one look at a map to know that Amsterdam is just a small part of the Netherlands. But as a traveler, you can often get tunnel vision about a country. The walls of which are defined by the material in your guidebook and the tips from fellow travelers who came before you.

Only the locals know what the real story is, and until you know them, you will never know it.

⊕

IN EARLY 2007 I moved to Bangkok for a month. I use that word specifically—*moved*—not *traveled* or *visited*, because I came to Bangkok this time with a purpose: to learn Thai before I visited Thailand's rural north. After spending close to five months roaming the tourist areas of Southeast Asia, I wanted something that felt a little more authentic, away from the backpackers and endless parties, and off the beaten path. An area with little development and few visitors, Isaan fit the bill. I figured learning Thai would help me get around and get to know the locals more. Bangkok was to be my base of operations.

And though I hated Bangkok since my first visit years ago with Scott, the capital with its proper "King's Thai" seemed like the best place to learn the language. Thailand has a bunch of regional dialects that, to the beginner, blend into each other. It's also a tonal language, so unless you hit the right tone in the right dialect exactly, it's often hard to make yourself understood. The good news is that "Bangkok Thai" is something of a universal currency in the country—even if it's not a local's "first language" way out in the provinces, chances are that you can make yourself understood.

Maybe I would grow to love Bangkok, I thought. There had to be something more than the pollution, traffic, and chaos I had seen as a tourist. The city had tens of millions of people. My first impressions of Prague had turned out to be wrong. Maybe I had just never seen the "real" Bangkok. My hope was that, as I learned more of the language and was better able to communicate, I could repeat my Amsterdam experience as well: I'd quickly find a place to live, make some local friends, get to know the city, and then, when the time came, move on, leaving behind a network of friends and acquaintances and local haunts to visit again.

Yet, over a week into my stay, I hadn't found my hook into the network I created in Amsterdam. There was no serendipity in Bangkok. No casino to find poker lovers. No other students in my class. I found little to do in the ways of tourist activities like museums, parks, or theater and the sprawl, heat, and pollution made it hard to just walk around and get lost. Each day, I'd wake up, go to class, look for new food vendors to try, visit some temples, and then go back to my guesthouse to play

Warcraft. It was as close as I'd ever come in my time on the road to the dog days of the work grind in my life back in Boston that I was doing my damnedest never to go back to.

Nothing seemed to just "happen" the way it had in Amsterdam. No matter what I did or how hard I tried, Bangkok wasn't giving up its mysteries to me, and I was starting to give up on it.

As I became more bored and melancholy, I eventually decided to extend my travels and return to Europe the following year. Travel was always the best escape from my boredom. I knew the road, what to expect, how it worked, and how to make friends on it. There I was never bored, never alone. And if I wasn't going to get out of Bangkok all that I was looking for or hoping for, I would move on to another of the world's amazing cities and try to find it there.

There was only one problem: I didn't have the savings to spend another summer in Europe.

I needed a job.

❀

IN SOUTHEAST ASIA, teaching English is one of the easiest jobs to get. Locals in the region want to learn the language in order to compete in the global market, and such demand meant anyone who grew up speaking the language (and a lot of those who didn't) are basically guaranteed a job.

Companies that sold English instruction to adults tended to pay well. If I taught for a few months and saved all my money (I had plenty of practice living cheaply), I could replenish my travel fund quickly and be back out on the road again in no time. It was the perfect plan.

I got a job at one of the larger language schools in the city. The school was on the complete other side of town, across the river in Pinklao. I moved into a closer guesthouse off of Khao

San Road. The backpacker haven was only about thirty minutes from my school in heavy traffic and I hoped closer proximity to other travelers might lift my spirits (and help me make some friends) while work filled my coffers.

But being closer to Khao San didn't change my situation. Each night I went out for a few hours and talked to people at the bars. But things were different now. Unlike them, I had work in the morning. I had responsibilities. I couldn't sleep late or be hungover. I wasn't in their world anymore. I had left the travel bubble. When I woke up in the morning, they would be onto their next destination.

While I was making countless five-hour friends, what I really wanted was something permanent since *I* was now permanent. I was trying to fill a void that was unfillable. For the first time, I understood why locals have no interest or patience for tourists and why they didn't want to spend their time getting to know them. Why would they give of themselves something they assumed I, as a traveler, wouldn't be able to give in return?

As one month blended into the next, and I made very little headway toward sinking roots into the Southeast Asian soil, a traveling friend of mine told me to contact her friend Zrs, a Filipino living in Thailand, who was also a teacher. "Maybe you two should meet, because I'm tired of hearing you complain about being bored," she said to me on Facebook. "You need to get out of your rut."

Zrs was short with cropped spiky hair and wore colorful printed shirts and jeans. When we finally met, we spent the entire night talking about girls, gaming (he, too, loved video games and had even custom-built a high-powered computer just to play them on), and the idiosyncrasies of life in Bangkok.

He quickly became my gatekeeper to life in Bangkok. Zrs

introduced me to a variety of local bars I had no idea existed. I met his friends, a mix of Thais and expats in the city. Together, these new figures quickly changed my life in Bangkok. The city opened up to me as if there was a secret code to the door that Zrs had entered on my behalf. Like one of those clubs you need to be sponsored by another member to join. His friends took me out to parties and a seemingly endless string of nightly networking events, dinners, and weekend outings.

My friend group expanded commensurately. There was Linda, an older American lady whose family owned a tourist map company and was sort of like the elder stateswoman of the city. There was Ryan, a flamboyantly gay Canadian whose job I never figured out. There was Katherine, an Australian who knew everyone; Laura, an American who always seemed to be planning a party; Florian, my German club promoter friend; and a string of others who all held day jobs at major corporations. Around all of them was a rotating cast of seemingly endless characters on the periphery.

Bangkok's expat community was incredibly intertwined. Meeting one person quickly led to meeting three others. It reminded me of the travelers network I'd been a part of as a backpacker moving from city to city, country to country, hostel to hostel. They were all strangers in a strange land, seeking out others like them to form a community—theirs more permanent than the backpackers'—of mutual support and understanding.

With all these events and new friends, living in Khao San was no longer a good option, because the longer I stayed the more I drifted from traveler to expat. Expat life is *real life*. And real life happened downtown.

I had to move.

⊕

EXPAT LIFE IS WEIRD. It has all the trappings of real life back home—responsibilities, routine, a desire for upward mobility, relationships, *commitments*—but with a layer of impermanence baked into it that is hard to ignore. Everyone here is doing a stint they don't know how long will last like soldiers on a tour of duty. A year? Two? A decade? Who knows! Maybe they will marry a local. Maybe work will take them somewhere else. Maybe they'll burn out and head home. Maybe they will stay forever. You never knew—and so everyone kept living as if they were on a long workcation. Never fully jumping into the deep end of settling down.

When I decided to move off Khao San Road to downtown Bangkok, I lucked out and found a cheap, furnished apartment in the same building Zrs lived in. The owners were friendly, offered laundry service, and taught me Thai. Even better the building was near my favorite bars and my new job at a company that taught high school kids how to game the SAT and other standardized tests as well as employees at large multinational companies how to write emails in English. I'm not sure what you call that kind of business, but it was the perfect job for an expat native English speaker with an MBA and no other immediately transferrable skills.

I worked there for the next few months, and though I essentially worked and lived the same 9-to-5 life I would have back in Boston, there was an excitement to life in Bangkok. Whereas Boston felt stale and unchanging, Bangkok was never boring. With all the expats and tourists coming and going, with the city's international vibe and revolving calendar of events, I found the constant flux and newness to everything the cure to failing into a rhythm that made me feel stale. It was actually the ideal combination of the working routine from my first weeks in

Bangkok learning Thai and the friend-filled extracurricular routines I'd developed in Amsterdam and in Ko Lipe the year before that.

After work, I'd go to Cheap Charlie's, the local expat bar, and make new friends from places around the world. Charlie's was an eclectic open-air bar on the side of one of the main streets, made from bamboo with a hodgepodge of phallic trinkets, weird toys, business cards from expats, and tables in front. At night, we'd clutter the sidewalks as the owner's wife hopelessly tried to contain the ever growing crowds. When the place finally burst at its seams, we'd leave to snake through the chaos of the streets and the ever-changing city landscape in search of Bangkok's nooks and crannies. It was like our own Thai version of *Shantaram*.

On weekends, we'd hit some of the big clubs. The clubs were one of the few places in Bangkok where locals, expats, and tourists mixed. One night, at a place called Bed, I met Justine. She was a journalist for the *The Nation*. Canadian born, half Chinese, Thai raised, Justine had cropped black hair and alabaster skin. She exuded confidence and intelligence. The gravity of her personality pulled everyone in and trapped me in her orbit like a moon around a planet. I was no exception.

We spent the night talking about books, politics, and journalism. I was mesmerized by the depth of knowledge she had on a variety of subjects. This was not a woman from whose orbit I was looking to free myself.

"I think I'm going to ask Justine out," I told Linda a few nights later at Cheap Charlies.

"Don't take this the wrong way, but she is out of your league."

"Why? You don't think I'm a catch?"

"Well, she's really classy and sophisticated and likes nice

things. She's not the kind to go backpack on Khao San with you. I just don't think you're the right match."

I had become accustomed back home to having limits placed on me, or being told what I could or couldn't be, and I'd even fought that inner self-talk while on the road, but I'd never quite encountered it so bluntly from others in my travels. Maybe that's one of the differences between spending time with travelers versus expats, I'm not sure.

What I was sure of was that I was not going to let Linda's estimation of me define how I felt about myself or what I might do. I was going to prove her wrong! This, too, was a surprise. Not because I had the guts to ask Justine out, but that I would ask her out at all. That was a decidedly non-nomad thing to do. You don't *go on dates* when you're backpacking around the globe, staying in hostels. You hang out and hook up. Dates were something you did when you were sticking around awhile. This was expat behavior.

Later that week, I ran into Justine at a networking event and asked her to dinner. She accepted. I made a reservation at one of the nicer Thai restaurants in the city. I forget what I wore, but I'll never forget the black dress and red lipstick she showed up in. She looked beautiful. Over dinner, we got lost in conversation. About *everything.* Linda was right, Justine did exude an air of sophistication. She was smart, educated, fiercely opinionated, and she shared many of my interests.

As the night ended, we kissed and she got in a cab.

"Call me," she said as she disappeared into the night.

This was where the adult life I had imagined existed. The excitement, the people, the hive of activity, the singular romantic connection. This is what I wanted.

Justine was my gateway into life in Thailand that I wouldn't have found as a backpacker—art openings, fancy restaurants, and regional foods, little hole-in-the-wall bars and clubs that go unnoticed. She taught me about the real Thailand and became my partner in crime.

However, as 2007 came to an end, work began to slow down. My company had expanded and there were too many teachers for too little work. Slowly, my hours kept shrinking and my feet began to itch accordingly. My original plan to stay a month had, in the blink of an eye, become eight. Without a good source of income anchoring me to the rhythms of daily Bangkok life, my mind once again began to wander to the road. According to my original plans, which I had almost entirely scuttled by this point, I was supposed to go to Australia right before Christmas. That was still three or four weeks away, but it was almost summer there anyway, so now seemed like as good a time as any to head south.

One night at a party, I broke the news to Justine: I was leaving for Australia three weeks earlier than planned. She did not take it well. She felt that I had made this decision without consulting her (there was truth to that) and exploded at me in our first—and only—fight. I think the fact that my trip was now a reality and not "something in the future" finally hit her. She had been discussing a future between us that ignored the fact I had told her about my travel plans from day one. I had just sped up the confrontation.

This is the eternal tension between the comfort and connection of the expat life and the restless, adventurous spirit of a nomad, of the perpetual traveler. They're like tectonic plates in a subduction zone. They can coexist quietly with each other for some length of time, but eventually the pressure they exert against each other will cause them to slip and one will get crushed under by the other, creating real damage at that epicenter of the break.

The traveler in me had come back and it was time to move forward. These two tensions couldn't coexist anymore. I knew this day was going to come. I had kept myself from getting too invested in my relationship for that very reason. I was taking things one day at a time. For Justine, a permanent resident of the city who was looking for something permanent, my natural nomadic sensibility blew up our relationship, because even she knew that there is no changing nature.

I was a nomad, and eventually, all nomads need to move on.

I HAD MIXED FEELINGS LEAVING BANGKOK.

When I first visited in 2005, I hated the city. As a tourist city, I still think it's terrible. There's not much to do or see. It's hard to get around. It's polluted. It doesn't have the endless activities for travelers that Paris or New York City offer.

As a tourist, I held my limited view of the city as gospel. There couldn't be any more to the place than what I saw. I had walked, I had seen the sights, and I had met the people. I had *seen* the city. If it was a bad tourist city, it must have just been a bad city.

This is something travelers do often. We pass through places, superficially making observations and generalizations as though we are experts and learned scholars.

We make sweeping judgments based on the limited interactions we have with locals, the weather, or some little mishap we are forced to endure. We see a snapshot of life and create a complete history from that one image.

On the road, you often hear people say things like, "The French are rude" or "I was in that city. It's boring there's nothing to do." But could an entire people be rude? Maybe there was something they did, as tourists, that got a rude response? Maybe they are boring and don't really know the city? Maybe they just missed something?

There are a million factors that can make or break a place. I hated Los Angeles until I really got to know it. To me, as a tourist, it was difficult to get around and I felt like there wasn't very much to do. But the more I visited, the more I realized there was a lot to do. That there isn't one Los Angeles, there are *seven* Los Angeleses, each with their own unique character. The problem was just that there wasn't a lot of *tourist* stuff to do.

Living in Bangkok taught me a similar set of lessons. I had made sweeping judgments based on limited experience. I painted a picture of the entire city from what I could see through the tiny peephole of my personal perspective. I hated a city that I really knew nothing about.

Needless to say now, but a handful of days in a city doesn't tell you much about the people or the place.

Bangkok might be the world's worst tourist city, but it was an incredible place to live in. The city I hated was now one I was going to miss tremendously. I had fallen in love with it.

Living around the world—first in Amsterdam, then in Bangkok, as well as Taipei and later Stockholm—taught me that if you slow down, you see more. It is only then that a place reveals its secrets to you. Slower travel also teaches you about yourself.

I moved to Bangkok not knowing anyone and I spent the first weeks alone on my computer. Yet, thanks to luck and Zrs, I made friends, got a job, learned the language, found a girlfriend, and created a social network. I navigated banking systems, rent, bills, and a culture I didn't understand.

Bangkok showed me that I could be self-reliant and independent. It taught me that I could shed the shy, nervous, and insecure kid I used to be. In Bangkok, I lived the life I had imagined in my head because for once I wasn't living out of the backpack into which I had smuggled all my baggage from home. I had settled in. I didn't let the past hold me down. I just became who I wanted. I discovered that I could love a place as a local, even if I didn't love it as a tourist. I could thrive in its out-of-the-way haunts and secret spots, the places a tourist wouldn't even think to look. I could feel at home on the other side of the world.

Bangkok taught me to slow down—a lesson I tell other travelers. You don't need to live in a place to learn something meaningful about it. But you do need more than a few alcohol-fueled days. It taught me that every place deserves a second chance, and that first impressions aren't always accurate.

And, most importantly, my experiences showed me that if I could start a life in Bangkok, I could start a life anywhere.

8

Love on the Road

We travel, initially, to lose ourselves; and we travel, next to find ourselves. We travel to open our hearts and eyes and learn more about the world than our newspapers will accommodate. We travel to bring what little we can, in our ignorance and knowledge, to those parts of the globe whose riches are differently dispersed. And we travel, in essence, to become young fools again—to slow time down and get taken in, and fall in love once more.

—PICO IYER

I WAS READY TO LEAVE BANGKOK, even at the cost of losing my budding relationship with Justine, because, when push came to shove, I was committed more than anything to my nomadism. Putting down roots was fine for a while, but I had no desire to put them down permanently.

It was a pattern that would repeat itself for years to come.

⊕

IN EARLY 2011, I was in Panama City and sharing a dorm room with a Finnish girl named Heidi. She was twenty-six, with typical Scandinavian features, and a carefree attitude toward the world. She waited tables during the summer and traveled in the winter. She was smart, extremely sarcastic, and knew how to playfully push my buttons.

She was also my opposite—opposed to technology, didn't have a camera or Facebook account, and only checked email once a week—so naturally we hit it off right away.

"Technology just weighs you down. I want to explore the way people used to communicate. With my undivided attention. I don't want to spend my entire trip behind a screen. That's not how one should travel," she explained, challenging everything I had turned into over the previous three years.

We began talking about going to Colombia. Heidi had found a couple to take her there on their boat by way of the San Blas Islands and she invited me to join them (but mostly her). The islands were supposed to be beautiful, remote, and unspoiled. A tropical paradise with white sand beaches, palm trees, and crystal blue water. I liked the idea of sailing to Colombia with Heidi. It was like a romantic fairytale. Here we were, two travelers meeting in a random country about to take a last-minute sailing trip through a tropical paradise.

Staring into a pair of blue eyes that could read me far better than I could read them, I went with my gut.

"Okay, I'll do it!"

We took the bus down to the port town of Portobelo where Heidi's friends were getting ready to set sail from. Beyond a few shops, a town square, and an old fort, there wasn't anything to do in Portobelo except launch boats out into the Caribbean Sea. To the west was the rest of Central America, immediately to the east was Colombia. If you found yourself in Portobelo, chances were you were going to one of those two places.

But, the day before we were set to sail, I got cold feet. It wasn't sailing, it wasn't Heidi, it wasn't Colombia. It was being afraid of going offline.

Because, unlike Heidi, I couldn't just walk away from technology and the internet.

In my years on the road, I'd learned quite a bit about the art of budget travel and met no end of people who shared my interests. I also knew there were thousands (maybe millions?) of people out there who wanted to do what I was doing but hadn't figured out how to pull it off.

When I came back home in 2008, I wanted to figure out the best way to use my travel experience to become a travel writer. I could see it all. I would discover unknown lands and report on them back home. I would offer insights from my firsthand experience with hostels, local culture, tourist traps, train, bus, and air travel. I would be a travel writer. A job that would keep me traveling. While I didn't know the first thing about being a writer, it seemed like a dreamy, adventurous job that would allow me to live out all those Indiana Jones fantasies from my youth.

Travel the world and get paid for it.

That would be the dream.

In 2008, that meant doing one thing: starting a blog. At first I thought of my website as more of an online résumé. I wanted my website to be a place where editors could see my writing and go, "Yeah, we want to hire that guy!"—and then send me places around the world.

Ironically, the path for this dream to become a reality would have to begin in the one place I was desperately trying not to come back to: home.

When I left Bangkok, my hop down to Australia was only a

pit stop. Two months removed from my expat life in Thailand, I was ensconced in what now felt like an even more foreign place—my childhood home—ready to begin my career as a travel writer. I registered NomadicMatt.com, sat down to build a website, and then realized I had no idea what I was doing.

The first several weeks were an absolute struggle. It was only with the help of a couple I met in Vietnam who were web designers, that I was able to learn html, the ins and outs of servers, web design, and how to interact effectively with people online. Sometimes even the simplest thing, like posting an image gallery to my site, could feel like hacking into an NSA database.

As the weeks turned into months, however, I got more comfortable with the technical aspects of running a website and spent more and more time writing stories about previous trips, giving advice on how to travel, and opining on matters of politics and travel. It was a lot of tedious, unrewarding work at first. But, gradually, as friends shared links to my blog and I found new topics to write about, I found that I was building a real audience that consisted more than just my parents refreshing the page in attempt to learn new things about me.

More than that, building my website gave my time away from the road a sense of purpose. I hadn't quit on my dream by coming home. By becoming a writer I was merely hitting the pause button to give myself the time and space I needed to make the most ideal version of my dream a reality—a life of traveling the world forever.

It took a while, to be sure, but by the end of 2009 things were trending in the right direction. While I was in New Zealand I caught a break. I saw a tweet from the writer of the *New York*

Times Frugal Traveler column on budget travel, asking if there were any bloggers out there who wanted to talk about how they made money.

"I do! I'd be happy to talk," I tweeted back. We exchanged messages. He agreed to interview me. In the middle of a small town in New Zealand as my tour group ate lunch, I walked outside and took a phone call that would change the course of my blog forever.

A few weeks later, I woke up to text messages and emails letting me know my website was down. Groggy and confused, I tried to load my website. It wouldn't work. While I was asleep, the *New York Times* had finally published the profile on me and sent so much traffic to my website it crashed. Repeatedly. For the entire day.

But my website was on the map now. I became a regular on radio and in print, giving interviews on the industry and budget travel. I spoke at conferences. I wrote articles and did interviews on other, much larger websites and blogs. My parents finally had something to point to—see our son isn't an itinerant loser, he's famous! *He's employed.*

Having a job quickly changed how I traveled. Sure, it removed the anxiety of not knowing how I would pay for the next leg of any trip, but it replaced that uncertainty with a different kind of anxiety. The kind that comes from responsibility. Before, I was a carefree traveler with no obligations and complete freedom. I could do what I wanted. Now, I had blogs to write, emails to answer, content to post, images to edit, and interviews to do. I loved my work and the ability to work anywhere, but it still came with deadlines and responsibilities.

I was no longer just in search of sandy beaches and fun bars, but also reliable WiFi and outlets with USB ports. Soon enough, my travels slowed to match the pace at which my workload increased. Day and night, I found myself preoccupied with the blog, with sustaining the readership I needed to feel like a success. I found myself falling more and more out of the moment. I couldn't just travel on a whim anymore. I was the guy in the back of the hostel in front of his computer while everyone else was sharing stories and making new friends. I was that guy *even when* I was out seeing the sights I'd come so far to see. Now, it wasn't, "What an amazing temple! Look at the detail on that sculpture! And these noodles are the best ever!" Now, it was, "This temple will make a great blog post. I better get a photo of that sculpture for my readers while the lighting is still good. I'd better remember how these noodles taste so I can write about them later." I was becoming a real travel writer, but at the expense of the nomadic life.

I had somehow managed to work myself into a real *job*.

But a job was the last thing I wanted. That was the whole reason I left Bangkok. And yet, here I was. Every hostel bunk became a cubicle. Every dinner was a fact-finding mission. Worse still, these works habits were starting to cost me relationships that I valued.

And, while I had struggled with the balance between working overseas and being a traveler true to his roots, Heidi was the one who forced me to choose between those two tensions— and showed me that they couldn't equally coexist.

As I thought about my trip, my mind raced through worst-case scenarios. What if something happened? We'd be out on the ocean and I wouldn't be able to fix anything. What if I missed an interview? An ad deal? A reader had a problem reaching out to me? What if, what if, what if!

Going offline when I ran an *online* business was more than I was comfortable doing. Don't get me wrong, I deeply wanted to travel with Heidi. That was the reason for running my blog in the first place: so I could travel; so I could see new things and make deep connections.

Yet this job that was supposed to give me freedom and flexibility had somehow managed to chain me to a virtual desk and made me afraid of the uncertainty that might come if I unchained myself from it. I just wasn't ready, or able really, to say "fuck it," which probably bothered me more than it bothered Heidi, but it was close.

"This is why I don't carry electronics or work when I travel. Travel is about letting go," Heidi said to me when I broke the news.

"I know but I've never done this before. I've never left my website for more than a day."

"Yes, but what do you think will happen?"

"I'm not sure," I said. "What if it goes offline?"

"Who cares? It will go back up. How can you write about things if you don't *experience* them?"

"I experience stuff. We've done a lot."

"I didn't mean literally," she said giving me a piercing look. "What I am saying is that when you started traveling, you were there 100 percent body and soul, right? When you are behind your computer working, you aren't. When you are always connected on Facebook, you aren't. When you spend twenty minutes trying to get a photo of that perfect sunset, you aren't. Seems like such a waste."

She was absolutely right. I had let work control me. She saw through all my excuses, all my fear. Afraid of losing her respect—and maybe even her, too—I told her I would clear some stuff away and I would meet her in Colombia. I still couldn't give

her everything she wanted, everything I'd originally committed to, but it felt like a decent compromise.

"You get there in seven days, right? Email me when you arrive and I'll hop on the next flight and meet you. This way," I
continued, "when I see you again, I'll be disconnected from the
web and we can enjoy Colombia the way it's meant to be."

"Okay. Sure," she said. I could sense the doubt in her voice.

"I'll see you in a week," I said, kissing her good-bye.

I never heard from her again. The week came and went. A
friend who was also on the boat said they landed safely. I knew
she had made it but my emails got no response. As I continued
around Panama, I checked my email each day in hopes that
eventually, one day, I would hear from her, but I never did.

Heidi was gone.

I understand why she ghosted. Here I was, a guy who chose
work and technology over sailing to Colombia with a beautiful
woman who liked him. We were fundamentally different people,
I guess, and she probably wanted someone who was more carefree.

I wish I could say it was a wake-up call, but it wasn't. It was
more like a self-inflicted kick in the nuts.

I had set out on my travels because I wanted to live instead
of work. But as my blog took off, I found that the same old work/
life problems were rearing their head again. If I wasn't sightseeing, I was working. Though it didn't make my trips less fun,
it did make them less carefree. There'd be no sudden sailing trips
to Colombia or time living on an island in Thailand anymore.

And because of my inability to unplug, I had missed an opportunity to spend time with a woman I really liked.

Worst of all, I'd forgotten one of my most important lessons,
one I've already written about in this book, and one that I tried

to get through to my readers on my blog: you control your plans; don't let your plans control you.

I'd started the blog in order to support my travel—in order to stay on the road even longer than I'd hoped when I set out. But slowly, I forgot *why* I was blogging, and found that blogging had become an end in itself. Ironically, the blog I started to support my travel had cost me the kind of opportunity that travel was supposed to be all about.

Because I couldn't learn to go with the flow.

Because I got tied to my plans.

I'd learned long ago to let go and let travel take you where it wants. Now, travel presented me with a choice to do something great with someone great. But I resisted. And travel, once again, taught me a hard lesson.

The lesson is that travel is all about seizing the opportunities in front of you—especially when they're opportunities to throw away your plans. As I realized that Heidi wasn't emailing back, I resolved to never forget why I began traveling in the first place. For the freedom and adventure. Heidi was the embodiment of everything I loved about travel and what pushed me to give it a go way back in the very beginning: she was a girl who had unhooked herself from modern life and let travel dictate her plans. I'd let plans dictate my travel—a mistake I vowed not to make again.

Somewhere, I'm sure Heidi agrees.

⊕

FINDING ROMANCE while traveling isn't hard. In the intense forge of travel, romances spring up rapidly. The same mind-set it takes to open yourself up to new experiences also helps you open yourself up to new people. Travel itself is romantic— passionate, scary, risky, all at once—and so it shouldn't be surprising that travel fosters romance. When we're on the road, we're often our best—or at least our most exciting—selves. For a brief time in our lives, we're people straight out of personals ads: curious, adventurous, full of new ideas and thrilling plans. *Anyone* seems sexier when setting out to explore a brand-new city than they do on the third of fourth morning of a five-day workweek.

Travel accelerates relationships, too. You can court, fall in love, and break up, all in a matter of a few days. In that way, there is almost paradoxically a perpetual singleness that goes along with traveling as well. It's very hard to build a long-term relationship when you are always on the move and never in one place long enough to build a lasting relationship with someone who lives there. And if you are dating another traveler, at some point it's time for you (or them) to move on. They go one way, you go another, and that's the end of your relationship.

In 2006, I was in Cambodia talking to some other backpackers in my hostel when a group of Swedish girls sat down next us. One caught my eye. Or, more accurately, I caught her eye. When we all went out later, she and I talked mostly to each other. Our conversation lasted four months and three countries. We didn't say good-bye until we were in Thailand, when she boarded a flight back to Stockholm and I stayed in Bangkok.

The following year, on a tour of Uluru in Australia, I struck up a conversation with a German girl. She became my travel partner for two months. I stayed at her place in Brisbane, and we met up again in Amsterdam the following year. We enjoyed one another's company—but after a few months, we realized, in a sense, that we weren't in the same story. We, too, went our separate ways.

Then there was the Austrian woman I dated while living in

Taiwan in early 2009. When my visa expired, and when she moved back to Vienna, our relationship fizzled out. I visited her in Vienna a few months later, but the truth was painfully obvious: she didn't want to leave Vienna, and I wasn't ready to stop traveling. Spending time together outside the context of travel, when she was at home but I wasn't, we both realized that the spark had gone.

This pattern repeats itself often on the road. I call these relationships "destination travel relationships." Without "life" getting in the way, relationships, like travel friendships, move quickly. You don't think about tomorrow. You don't think about your partner's past. You simply enjoy each other's company for as long as it will last. Maybe that's four months in Southeast Asia. Maybe it's a few weeks up the east coast of Australia. Or maybe it is just that week together in Amsterdam.

Destination relationships give travelers a chance at human contact, but without all the messy emotions that so often get involved. They have a clear start and end date. There are no messy breakups. Often, because these relationships tend to end amicably, you can still be friends after. I still talk to the girls I've dated on the road. We shared special times together, and then we both moved on. No hard feelings. The logistics of a destination relationship—the realities of a planned route, bus timetables, flight schedules, visa expirations—got in the way. What really brings those relationships to an end is the mutual, if unspoken, agreement that both of you are more committed to traveling than to each other. And that's fine—there's no better recipe for an unhappy long-term relationship than settling down before both partners are fully ready. The beauty of relationships on the road is that everyone shares the same set of priorities. And if those priorities don't make long-term love possible, they do enable a lot more honesty about what we're really looking for.

I grew up thinking that there's something wrong with a relationship that both parties understand to be fleeting. Even as college students and twentysomethings participate in hookup culture, we've still internalized the sort of goal-oriented, puritanical message that America is so good at drilling into our heads: the point of hooking up is to ultimately find someone to be with forever, to stop hooking up and start settling down. A breakup, after all, means that something has broken— relationships that end are failures. It took me a while to get over this mind-set, to learn to see the momentary beauty in relationships that everyone involved agreed were fleeting. Impermanence can be beautiful, too.

It took time for me to learn that lesson, and to recognize the difference between when something was fleeting and something was for real.

When I was in Florence, I was sitting in my hostel's large courtyard drinking cheap but delicious wine with Peter when I noticed a beautiful girl across the courtyard who, eventually, noticed me, too. Her name was Anna. She was sitting with seven others—two girls and five guys—all of whom, including Anna, were from Valencia, Spain, had just graduated university, and were getting ready to go to a club.

"Would you like to join us?" they asked in better English than my broken Spanish, when I walked over to their table with my friend and we introduced ourselves.

"Of course," we said.

While walking to the club, which ended up being right down the street, I did my best to flirt with Anna in the limited time we had before house music drowned out our voices. She smiled and said something in Spanish before turning to her friends and entering the club with them.

Inside, however, Anna warmed up to me. And as the night wore on, she started talking more, and her body language changed. When we got back to the hostel at the end of the night, we raided the kitchen for late-night snacks and took them out into the wide courtyard where we ate and talked and then kissed.

"Where is your room?" she asked, pulling away momentarily. "I'm with my friends. Let's go to your room."

My dorm was mostly empty and the two guys in the far corner snored so loudly that I don't think they noticed us come in. In the morning, after Anna left, I apologized for "coming in drunk so late." They shrugged. That's how it goes on the road. And it should have been the end of the story, if I'd known better.

Later that day, Anna, her friends, and I toured Florence. We wandered to the Ponte Vecchio, the famous covered bridge. The bridge was crowded with foot traffic and lined with shops that were braced perilously over the Arno River. I wondered how it had all stayed intact for six and a half centuries.

With a limited budget, all we could afford was walking and people watching, splurging only occasionally on gelato to grease the wheels. We watched sharp-dressed Italians zoom by on scooters, and we watched tour groups gawk at the sights. We strolled to Piazzale Michelangelo and we gazed down on the town and its red-colored roofs.

But the more I tried to talk to Anna, the less interested she became. It was a classic case, exacerbated by the way the road brings you in touch with so many new faces each day and encourages you to compare and take stock of your options: if I was so interested in her, then surely she could do better. The more someone wants you, after all, the less you want them. This experience brought out a host of old insecurities. What did I do wrong? Was I coming across as too needy? Did I not know a drunk hookup when I saw one?

Deep down I knew I wasn't going to see Anna again, but it still stung. Fortunately, the hurt we often feel in situations like these is a sign that we're learning something important. What I was learning was not to make relationships on the road into more than they were, into more than the moment called for. It's okay to be transitory, and it's okay to let go—to stop trying so hard to make everything last beyond its expiration date. Just for a moment, I'd caught the eye of a foreign beauty, and in the span of a day, I'd been through love, lust, and the pain of rejection.

That's not to say relationships on the road can't work, but *someone* has to change the direction of his or her life to make that a reality. Someone needs to say, "Okay, I'll move to your place" or "Okay, I'll go with you to that country." Someone has to cede the wheel or the map, or at least be willing to share it. And, when the whole point of traveling is to enjoy the freedom of deciding where and when you get to go, not many people do that.

I've met couples who have found love on the road, traveled together, and then settled down when one of the partners agreed to a long-term move. Or they started a new life together, finding a new city that neither wanted to leave. You come together when your paths temporarily cross but, if you stick to your original plans, they will surely uncross again.

That's how it was for me, the compass was constantly driving me away from whatever fate might have aligned. Travel was my only love. When push came to shove, I always chose the road and the excitement and adventure that awaited. It was why Justine and I split, it was why I knew there was no future for me in Vienna or in Australia.

But by the time I met Samantha at the end of 2011, in the wake of having blown it with Heidi months earlier, I finally began to accept that the fleeting nature of travel romance was all too fleeting for me. I wanted something deeper and longer lasting.

⊕

"WE'RE GOING TO GRAB drinks if you want join us," I wrote back to Samantha. She was traveling the region with her friend, Kira. Like me, they had a travel blog; when they saw I was in Bangkok, they emailed me to meet up.

"Meet us on Khao San Road," I replied

"Sure," she wrote back, "We'll meet you there."

I was meeting some blogger friends at one of the roadside buckets bars on Khao San Road. Over the previous three years, most of my new friends had come from the blogging community. It had been strange running into an online friend for the first time in Thailand, or Florence, or the Outback, and feeling as if you'd known them for months or years. But that's the nature of travel in a networked world, and I got used to it.

Samantha and Kira showed up about thirty minutes after the rest of us arrived. Samantha was short, with beautiful blue eyes and a wide smile. Originally from Oregon, she was affable, funny, and gregarious. As the night went on, we talked until we were the only two people left at the bar.

The next morning, Samantha joined the rest of us as we talked over our coming trip to Ko Chang, an island near the coast of Thailand. In all the years I'd been in Thailand, I'd never gone and thinking back to how those backpackers in 2005 told me it was paradise, decided it was finally time to see it.

Samantha listened intently, then came with us as we went for drinks and to see some sights. Kira's boyfriend was in town, and she and Kira had been fighting recently, so she had lots of free time on her hands to do with as she pleased. When she mentioned that, it was clear their travel styles were diverging and she was kind of done being a third wheel, so I invited her to come with us to Ko Chang.

"Come! It will be fun," I said to her. "We're only going for a few days. It will be a good way to help your stress. Sometimes you just need some time away."

"Let me think about it," she said.

A few hours later, she called me. "Okay! I'm in. I'll go!"

Samantha was beautiful, smart, and adventurous. In her, I found the travel partner I wanted. Samantha went with the flow and wanted to meet people. We shared a bungalow, went to the beach, and went snorkeling. As we laughed, drank, and partied, Samantha slowly began to relax.

From Ko Chang, Samantha and I went back to Bangkok, where she and Kira officially went their separate ways for the sake of their friendship, and then we went to Chiang Mai. In Chang Mai, Samantha, having been there recently, became my food guide. We wandered markets, tried khao soi, frequented the famed Dada Kafe for breakfast each morning, and, during the Sunday market, divided and conquered food halls, bringing back random assortments of food to our table to try.

From there, we went to Kuala Lumpur and then flew to Cambodia in the new year. We were going to spend a few weeks in the beach town of Sihanoukville. Earlier in the year, an email from a publishing house had landed in my inbox. An editor there had found my website and wanted to turn my ebook, *How to Travel the World on $50 a Day,* into a book. A real book.

I replied. The offer was real. Papers were signed—and the work began. Slowly. A blog is easy. An ebook is easy. A book is *hard.* As the March deadline got closer, I began to stress out about finishing it. There was a lot more research than I had originally expected, and I had underestimated the level of detail I'd have to add to the ebook.

Thankfully, Samantha was all too happy to hang out in Cambodia while I finished writing. We had been traveling together for four months, and she was also ready to take a break.

We'd spend the mornings working before heading to the beach or on another activity before I'd write again after lunch. At night, we'd meet with a few people for drinks and dinner. As we began to stay longer, we became regulars at a few places and friends with the owners and staff.

As the clock ticked down on the due date for my book, Samantha left to visit Vietnam with her mom. When you are with someone 24/7 and dealing with the stresses of the road, your relationship ages faster. We'd never officially given ourselves the boyfriend/girlfriend titles, but we were for all intents and purposes a couple. For the first time in many years, I began to think about not leaving, about not wanting her to leave, about not wanting there to be an end to this, to us. And I worried that her going to Vietnam while I stayed in Cambodia to finish the book would be, like so many relationships before, the beginning of that end. Not only that, but once I was done, I would be returning to the States to speak at some conferences, and put in another round of edits, while she was headed home to Oregon a few months after that to help take care of a sick uncle.

Weeks later, we met up back in Bangkok one last time before

I left. I didn't want to leave her. I didn't want to say good-bye. So instead, I tried to turn it into a "See ya later." I invited her to Japan and to Sweden with me (where I wanted to spend the summer).

"Ohh, you're going to pay for the trip?" she said sarcastically, laughing at the suggestion.

"Yeah, I want to see you," I replied. "You've always wanted to go to Japan, and we can find a place in Stockholm for a few months."

"Let me think about it," she said. The next day I left for home.

Unlike our first trip to Ko Chang, this time there would be no enthusiastic phone call telling me she was in. Our conversations became less frequent. And when she didn't call on my birthday I knew that she was out. Though she called a few days later and I countered that I'd go anywhere she wanted to go, she said no.

I didn't understand at first. We had left on good terms. What had changed since I left?

With distance, of course, nothing had changed. Only the context from which I was looking. Whatever love we'd had for one another only existed inside the travel bubble—the self-contained world of hostels and beaches and sightseeing. Outside that bubble, back in the real world, our feelings for one another had no foundation. Outside of the travel bubble, our love had withered and died.

As it was destined to.

She just knew it before I did.

⊕

WHEN I FIRST STARTED TRAVELING, I was worried about making friends and finding my groove, but I never really thought about being alone. When 2012 came to an end, being alone is all I really wanted. I wanted to go off the grid and relax before my book came out in January. It had been a trying year, and I was still depressed about Samantha. I needed an escape. Some place where I could clear my head.

I chose Southern Africa. It offered everything I wanted—weeks camping in nature disconnected from the world—and delivered on all of it, until one evening in Namibia as I stared out at the watering hole in Etosha and the setting sun turned the sky a fiery red and purple. Around me were families, friends, couples. I was there by myself on purpose, but looking around at all these people who seemed to have someone, who were enveloped in the joy of sharing this magical moment together, I suddenly felt very alone. True loneliness hit me in the face like a ton of bricks. And the more I sat with that emotion, the more I understood that I was done being alone.

Sure, there is value in going solo: You have no master but yourself. Your time and thoughts are entirely your own. But the way all those couples and families looked as they soaked in the dazzling African sunset made it seem like they were enjoying the experience far more than I was, simply by virtue of the fact that they could share it with the people they loved. I always thought that was such a cliché, until the moment when it was the whole truth and nothing but the truth. I had first traveled to escape being easily defined; now I had fallen into the trap of being easily defined . . . as a traveler. Travel had become my cubicle, and I was in it by myself.

Watching that sunset was a kind of painful joy: joyful, because of how full of beauty the world seemed just then, and painful, because I couldn't turn to someone I cared for to see the same joy in their eyes.

Where was my special someone? Where was someone to put

my arm around? Someone to talk with about what we had seen during the day? Someone to share in my work or in the excitement of seeing an elephant?

I didn't think of Etosha. I thought of Samantha.

I thought back to the last time we'd spoken. I had asked her if we could have another chance to see if our relationship would work. She told me she had been dating someone else, and wasn't ready to jump back into a relationship with me. Our story had ended. That talk was the epilogue.

I think what bothered her was that we were at two stages of life. Family was always important to her. She always joked about having five kids—and in most jokes there is a kernel of truth. Yet, as much as I wanted a relationship, I didn't want kids. A nomad can't have kids. A nomad carries a backpack, not a Baby-Björn. I wanted *negative* kids. I wanted zero bowlines to me and the dock. I wanted zero obligations to anyone but myself . . . and maybe a travel partner.

In retrospect, we weren't right for each other, but all relationships impart some wisdom in their disintegration. In ours, I came to realize the idea of a family might be far away, but the idea of wanting someone else was front and center.

In Etosha, I thought about Samantha and the happiness I experienced traveling with her. I no longer desired to wander cities or gaze upon African sunsets alone. I wanted to gaze at a familiar face. I wanted to share moments. I was tired of having to start over in each new city and make new friends.

I wanted *someone*. I lacked the deep connections that you get when you grow roots in a place. Trees grow tall and powerful because they are rooted deep in the soil, but I was still a seed blowing in the wind. I wasn't grounded by anything. I thought

I had put down roots in the world of travel, but it was only keeping me rootless. I decided then and there that it was time to settle down, make friends, and then who knows what from there.

But it turned out stopping was a lot harder than I thought.

9

Burning Out, Coming Home

A good traveler has no fixed plans, and is not intent on arriving.

—LAO TZU

I THINK I'M DONE, I said to Matt over drinks in Brisbane. He had relocated from Perth while I was traveling across Australia.

After eighteen months on the road, I began to experience a sensation that, until this point, I'd only read about: travel burnout.

Travel was no longer fun. It was *work*.

There's this perception—from both travelers and nontravelers alike—that travel is all excitement, all the time. Before I'd set off, I'd even indulged that perception myself. It's natural to only imagine the good bits to come. We do that with our future as well as our past. Think back to some of the highlights from your past: how many of them include waiting in line at the grocery store, holding a pole on the bus, being stuck in traffic, filing your taxes? We edit those sorts mundane moments out of our past. But we also preemptively edit those sorts of things out of our future. We treat anticipated travel like a highlight reel that plays in advance. It let's our imagination play through all the fun scenarios we think we'll experience when we travel. That's why the planning phase is always so much fun.

Burnout can seem like the ultimate in ingratitude. What's there to be tired of? You have complete freedom. You're on an adventure that most people only dream of taking. You are seeing famous attractions, meeting people from all over the world, trying new cuisine, learning new languages. You don't have any responsibilities. You get to do whatever you want, whenever you want. There's nothing to get in your way of any of your craziest desires or whims. And what, you're *over it?*

So you'll ask yourself, like I asked myself: *Why am I not enjoying this more? What's wrong with my trip? What's wrong with me?*

The truth is that our anticipations, and our memories, have a way of holding only the most striking parts of an experience— the parts that *don't* cause burnout. Talk to anyone who has just returned from Disneyland with children and they will tell you tales of a congested hellscape full of long lines, screaming children, arguing parents, and overpriced everything. Talk to them a year later about that same trip, and all you'll hear about is princess breakfasts and memories and funny stories. They'll probably even show you pictures the kids took with their favorite Disney characters.

It's the same way with long term travel. When you're planning a trip, all you see is excitement. You see the parties, the sightseeing, the new friends and food you'll try. You create a highlight reel of your trip even before you've boarded your first flight. When you're planning your trip and taking ownership of your adventure, you can't imagine that there will be a downside.

Why would you? You're going on an adventure, and adventures are inherently thrilling—at least they're supposed to be. Who's ever heard of a boring adventure? A shitty adventure? A disappointing adventure? The possibility never even enters your head when you're in the planning stage. Your head is full of all the life-changing things you're going to do, and how your adventure is going to be better—not worse—than wherever you are right now.

When you're creating your highlight reel, you don't think about the long, boring hours you're going to spend on tiny buses. You skip over the delays at airports or the train strikes that leave you stranded. You don't think about snorers in hostel dorms, food poisoning, dirty accommodations. You think about making friends with the locals, not about fending off touts and scammers, or losing your wallet. You think of an experience that will supply memories for a lifetime, not of all the tiny hassles that suck energy and joy out of your life.

In this way, anticipation works just like memory—editing out the boring bits, glossing over the pain and frustration, turning the tedious into the glamorous. The great travel writer Paul Theroux said that "travel is only glamorous in retrospect." But what holds true for looking back also holds true for looking ahead—travel is glamorous in prospect, too.

You forget that travel can settle into a routine just as easily as office life can. Get up, eat a terrible hostel breakfast (burnt toast and cornflakes, usually, and if you've found some peanut butter left in the jar, you're winning), sightsee, meet travelers, go out at night, sleep off your hangover, pack up, find your bus, and head to the next town to do some variation of it over and over again, for who knows how long. Those beautiful places you set out to see are still there—but they've become the backdrop to the same old cycle. It's as if you stop seeing them so vividly, like the scenery behind a *Mario Kart* race. The setting for each level is unique, but all you really see is the track.

And the longer you travel, the more the novelty fades, and the more the routine hardens into boredom.

You get sick of constantly trying to find your bus or hostel in countries whose language you don't speak. You're tired of making plans from scratch each day. You're worn out of seeing new friends take the bus out of town, never to be heard from again. The quotidian parts of life that you take for granted at home— finding food that won't make you sick, figuring out where to clean your laundry, communicating about bus schedules or menus—become tedious chores.

You have to learn a brand-new set of social norms at each stop. You have to restart your life again and again, in a new place and with new people. As much as the backdrop changes, nomad life can come to resemble an unending Groundhog Day.

And when it does, the fun of being able to do whatever you want wears off. You don't want to see one more fucking temple or waterfall. You don't want to invest time in getting to know one more person who is just going to disappear. You don't care about other travelers, where they are from or where they are going. You don't want to unpack and pack every day. You don't want to pretend to sleep through two drunk people having sex in the bunk above you.

All you want to do is stay in one place, watch Netflix, and relax. You crave the monotony of the life you left. A nice bed, someone to fully understand the words you are saying, someone to stay longer than a day, some consistency and dependability.

One day you reach your limit.

Congratulations: you're burned out.

⊕

WHEN I BEGAN MY TRAVELS, a million and one fears and worst-case scenarios ran through my mind. What if I couldn't make it? What if I couldn't find friends? What if I got so lost I couldn't find my way back? What if I got sick? What if I ran out of money?

And I blew those fears out of proportion, because for some reason I kept neglecting the obvious solution if any of them came to be. Barring the absolute worst-case scenario, I could always come home. If it didn't work out, there was always the next flight home.

People rarely think about that option.

They assume that once you're on the road, you're stuck. That when it doesn't work out there's nothing that can be done.

It's ironic, when you think about it. Being a traveler is about being free—and yet it's possible to commit to the nomadic life so deeply that you forget you're always free to go home. You forget that you can say, at any time, "You know what? I miss my home and my friends. I will scream if I see another hostel. It turns out that I'm done with budget travel for now, and the next time, I'll try something more comfortable, even if that means traveling for a shorter period of time. I've had enough for now. I'm going to go home."

You're free to stop. But stopping seems like the least free thing you can do.

It feels like an admission of failure.

You'd be surprised how resistant a committed nomad can be to making that admission. I wish they wouldn't be. We travel to become better people, and one of the ways we do that is by learning about ourselves along the way. One of the things travel sometimes teaches you is that you don't want to travel anymore. There's nothing wrong with coming home.

There's no shame in admitting that travel can be hard. It's not all rainbows and unicorns—it's routine, frustration, stress, and disappointment, too. And if you find those feelings swelling up inside of you—if you find that the thought of one more temple is going to make you snap, that is the sign that you need to make a change.

I left Bangkok to continue my journey, but there, wandering around Australia—first up the West Coast, then down through the center and then back up the coast—I found I had little desire to engage with the people I met on the road.

I saw fresh recruits come through the hostel door and—while once I would've rushed to swap stories with them and offer advice—now I only wanted to tell those kids was to get off my lawn or go to my website if they wanted to hear what I had to say. I yearned sometimes for a hotel, where none of these other people were. Where I had privacy and niceties and a robe to put on.

As days turned into weeks, I began to feel as if the magic in my relationship with travel was gone. That I was simply going through the motions. The scenery was beautiful. I met a few people I really clicked with, including a German girl who would travel with me on and off for the next few years. But, for the most part, I resented the young college kids who seemed to be vapid and only concerned about partying. The backpackers here seemed different than the ones I had previously met in Europe and Southeast Asia, and I didn't want any part of them.

Or maybe it was just me who had changed. I felt older than all of the other backpackers I met—not in calendar years, but mentally older. I had already "been there and done that."

I found myself repulsed by the newbies filled with optimism and a desire to drink themselves stupid. It seemed so fake and phony to me. Where was the desire to learn about other cultures? To sightsee? To meet locals? Where was the authenticity?

Whenever someone invited me to go get drunk on the beach with them, I almost had to stifle my gag reflex. I was tempted to say, "I've been doing that for the last year. Isn't there anything else we can do?"

But, as far as the others were concerned, there wasn't. They weren't jaded yet—it was all new to them, even as it was getting painfully old to me.

By the time I met Matt in Brisbane, I had hit my breaking point.

"If you don't like traveling, don't do it." Matt said. "You don't need to prove anything. You've been gone close to eighteen months. Go relax back at home, and come back when you're ready. The world will always be here."

"I know, but I just feel like I'm giving up. I'm so close to New Zealand and the end. Am I just being impulsive?" I asked Matt. He should know—at that point, he'd been a world traveler for nearly five years, and had completed an itinerary much like mine two times already.

"Nah man," Matt replied. "You have to follow your gut. Traveling is like a relationship. There are going to be ups and downs. The trick is to know when it is truly over. It sounds to me like it's truly over for you right now."

"I know, but I'm torn. On the one hand, I love traveling. On the other, the thought of traveling longer makes me sick. I don't care about the people I meet or the things I do. I don't want to see museums or sit on the beach anymore."

"You can stay, but you're going to be miserable. There's nothing wrong with going home. Or just stay put in one place, recharge your batteries, and go back out again, if you still want to travel. But don't rush yourself. What's the point of traveling if you don't want to do anything?"

As burned out as I was, home seemed equally boring. I sipped my beer and pondered Matt's advice.

The next day, on impulse, I decided to listen to Matt. I booked a flight home. I didn't check the price. I didn't look for a way to hack it with miles. Matt was right. The world would always be there. I was done. In two weeks, after eighteen months away, I'd be home.

⊕

I RETURNED TO THE United States in January 2008, for the first time with no plans of going back out, with no job, no money, and, worst of all, to living with my parents.

At first, home was fun. It was exciting to be back. I went to my favorite restaurants, visited the bars I used to frequent, did some sightseeing around Boston, and held some "Welcome Home" parties to catch up with my friends.

I saw my old home with new eyes. The mouthwatering taste of my favorite sushi restaurants, breakfast joints, and sub shops. The rhythm of conversation in my favorite bars. Even the clamor of the Big Dig, Boston's massive highway project sounded like home. Reentering life in my old city felt natural, easy, seamless. The city was like comfort food for my bad breakup with travel. Plopping down in my old bed and wrapping myself in my blanket was exactly what I needed.

But once the odd excitement of comfort wore off and I found myself with lots of time on my hands while my friends were at work, boredom set in again. I'd escaped Boston to escape the pattern and routine of my life there, and now I was falling back into it sooner than I had imagined. Home had remained frozen during my time away. My friends had the same jobs, were going to the same hangouts, and mostly doing the same things. The bars were full of the same kinds of people and playing the same kinds of music. The city had the same old stores and the same old construction work.

What had excited me in the moment of return was now a reminder of all the reasons why I left in the first place and how I had changed on the road. Nostalgia had turned into monotony, which had turned into stasis, which had turned into atrophy. All in the matter of a few weeks.

There's a post-trip depression that happens when you return home. A jarring sense of whiplash as you get pulled back into your old life. As you leave for your trip, you're full of excitement, wonder, and zest. You're going to conquer the world. Soon, you're moving a thousand miles a minute as you explore the world, taking in every activity you come across. That momentum continues when you first get home and then all of a sudden, bam! The music abruptly stops.

Everyone leaves the party and there's nothing more to look forward to. No more adventures. No more new friends. New food. New flights. You're home now. This entire existence and way of life just ceases in a flick of the fingers.

Your friends don't want to hear about that time you were sailing the Pacific while they were sitting in traffic. They don't want to hear another story set in a place they've never been to and featuring people they'll never meet. They can't understand why you are so uncomfortable being back.

"How was your trip?" they ask.

And as you explain your life their eyes glaze over, and you

begin to wish you were back at the hostel bar—any hostel bar—talking with a circle of other travelers, people who have dedicated their lives to adventure, people who share your same restlessness and wanderlust.

Going back to the same old routine I had fought so hard to leave felt like dying. I had made a life for myself in Bangkok. I had learned Thai. I had camped in the Outback, explored cities in Europe, and spent a month barefoot on an island in Thailand. I had changed. I had become more confident, more outgoing, more adventurous. I had outgrown my old life—and now I found myself suddenly back in it again. Home was supposed to be the happiest place in the world. And yet, here I was, feeling like I'd left home for nothing, feeling as if I didn't fit but was still condemned to spend the rest of my life here. And, what made it worse, was that no one around me understood why I felt sad or depressed. I was without support.

One night, I was out with my friends and grappling with thoughts like these. Across the bar, I saw a guy wearing a red shirt with a golden star in the front. It's the Vietnam flag shirt, and nearly every backpacker in Southeast Asia has it. It's up there with the Laos beer singlet or the "same same but different" shirt. It's worn as a badge of honor. A symbol that you're a member of the travel tribe.

Here was a traveler. Someone I could speak to. Someone to take back to those days on the road, even if just for a moment. I decided to strike up a conversation and walked over to him.

"Hey man! Nice shirt. Did you get that backpacking in Southeast Asia?"

"Yeah, how did you know?"

"I got that same shirt in Vietnam, too. I just came back from my trip a few weeks ago."

"Where did you go?" he said ecstatically.

"Everywhere! I was there for nearly a year."

Like two soldiers who find each other amid a sea of "civilians" who will never understand what we've been through, we swapped war stories from the road, trying to see where our trips overlapped, what bars we remembered, and which places we each knew the other didn't. We were playing that immortal game of "I'm a better traveler because. . . ." We traded stories about "hidden gems" the other one missed, and off-the-beaten-path highlights. But though games like these might look competitive, they're really friendly, full of the mutual recognition of kindred spirits who share the same priorities in life. When I explained my feelings about being back home, he understood just what I was going through—he'd been through the same thing when he returned.

After about ten minutes of conversation, I wished him well and went back to my friends, happy to have met someone who shared my experience and understood how I was feeling.

"Who was that guy?" my friends asked.

I explained the meaning of the shirt and about travel in Southeast Asia. Their confused reaction—why was I talking to a stranger about a shirt?—cemented the sadness I was feeling inside about not being understood.

Do you remember the movie *The Curious Case of Benjamin Button*? There's a line from that movie that has always stuck with me: "It's a funny thing about coming home. Nothing changes. Everything looks the same, feels the same, even smells the same. You'll realize what's changed is you."

The road had changed me more deeply than I originally thought.

I had this fire in me now, and even if I had burned out on travel, the fire was still smoldering enough in me to make home uncomfortable. Travel had made me better. My time meeting people and living overseas had given me the confidence to talk to strangers in bars even back home—something the old Matt would never have done.

Being back home made me realize that I hadn't gotten travel out of my system—no, in fact, I wanted even more. I wanted to keep going, just differently than before.

I had broken out of the American Dream bubble and seen that there was a big world out there filled with possibility and adventure. Like an addict, I wanted it all the time and I couldn't understand why no one else did. I couldn't understand why no one wanted to go beyond the same bars and restaurants each week. Why no one wanted to go on a road trip or take an adventure.

I was right back where I'd started but now I was a different person, one who could tolerate middle-class America even less. I had plenty of time to think those thoughts in front of my computer at the temp job I had gotten with the help of a cousin. (It didn't help that it was another cubicle job in the health care field—literally back where I had started.) I bashed my head against the keyboard. I refused to let my life fall back to where it was before.

"Why the fuck did I come home? Why was I so rash?"

I could have kicked myself. I should have kept going. I should have just stopped in Australia for a bit. I hadn't even bothered to try to repair my relationship with travel. I just ran away from it, and now I was regretting that decision.

I didn't take this year-long trip around the world just to end up right back where I started. I took it to become a new, more confident person with interesting stories to share with people.

Now that I had become that person, how was I right back where I started? Life had remained frozen in time waiting for me, and I didn't want any part of it. The new me couldn't fit into my old life. There was nothing wrong with Boston, my friends, work, or this life. But it was no longer what I wanted.

My website and the online community I found through it became my outlet. It allowed me to pretend that I was just on a break from traveling to get my bearings. I was just on a break that would soon end, and then, shortly after my twenty-seventh birthday, I booked a one-way flight to Europe, called up my boss in Bangkok to see if I could teach again, and prepared to leave in August.

It was time to get back to where I belonged.

⊕

HERE'S THE THING ABOUT travel burnout. It happens over and over again. You will *always* hit a wall.

Burnout isn't a problem you can solve, but a condition you must learn to deal with, because the conditions that caused you to burn out in the first place never go away.

In fact, the longer you travel, the more often this will happen. Anyone who travels long term will get burned out at some point. But what happens if your trip doesn't have a start and stop date? As I became a permanent nomad, traveling was just what I did. The world was my office. It became my routine.

And sometimes it sucked.

Because while you keep getting older, to borrow a phrase

from Matthew McConaughey, new travelers stay the same age. Actually, that's not true, they get younger. They have the same wide eyes and ask the same questions you've been asked a thousand times before. They want to party. They want to make new friends with everyone. Individual backpackers may come and go, but as a group they never change.

They don't change the way you're changing. You began to change how you travel: seeking fewer but deeper relationships; trying to drink less; wanting to avoid the same conversation you've had a thousand times over. You're just tired of restarting all the time.

As one year rolled into two, two became five, five became seven, I grew out of dorm rooms, pub crawls, and knocking off a to-do list of the top attractions in a city. I got tired of living out of a suitcase. I wanted to go deeper and began to see fewer destinations and spend more time in the ones I did. I began to seek out friends I made on my earlier trips more than I tried to make new ones.

I grew to understand that burnouts were a natural part of travel. I didn't need to fight it them. I didn't need to make the rash decision to run home, only to regret it and then go away again.

No, I learned that like everything in life, there will be ups and downs. One doesn't need to travel all the time to live a life of adventure. The purpose of travel was also the purpose of flexibility: to create a life of your own desire.

When you feel burned out from travel, you don't have to run away, you just need to stop, relax, and stay still. Because desire is not an unlimited wellspring, but a battery that needs to be recharged. Constant travel drains that battery. So if it happens to you—and it will—listen to your heart. Stop and relax. Take stock and take care of yourself. Because if you don't, if you make my mistake, you'll end up sitting at a desk wondering if you'll ever get back out there again, and that is the worst feeling in the world for a nomad.

10

Going Back Out

No man ever steps in the same river twice.

—HERACLITUS

YOU'VE PROBABLY HEARD those words from Heraclitus before, even if you didn't know who said them. They're true for two reasons: the river is always changing, and you're always changing. To imagine that you can freeze the world around you at any given moment is as foolish as imagining you can stop the flow of a river. And to imagine that you can stop yourself from changing is a recipe for unhappiness. True happiness, and true wisdom, lies in embracing change as a fact—*the* fact—of life.

I'd tried to internalize this wisdom. In fact, it's part of the nomad's code, in a sense—always on the move, meeting new friends in new places, never content to settle down. You can't be a nomad for as long as I was without some willingness to embrace change as a basic expectation of your life. I thought I'd learned at least *that* lesson by the time I came back home.

And yet, the change I observed in myself still almost shocked me. Boston, as I've mentioned, hadn't seemed to change that much on the outside. My friends and family hadn't changed in any remarkable way. But I felt, in these familiar surroundings, like an entirely new person.

It almost felt like that scene in the movie *Cast Away,* when Tom Hanks has finally escaped off the desert island and is at a reception in his honor. The abundance of food, the luxurious setting . . . all of it feels foreign to him. There's a similar scene in *The Hurt Locker.* Jeremy Renner's character has come home from a tour of duty in Iraq and we see him at a big box store, looking up bewildered at the fluorescent lights and the towering stacks of *stuff.*

He has only one response. He reenlists. He misses the adrenaline. He'd rather risk death than deal with the mundanity of life.

That's what it was like being home. It was bigger than just the stuff that surrounded me. When I first left, I had a vague sense that there was more to life than what I had experienced in Boston. Now I knew for certain. I had tasted it. Every time I felt overwhelmed, I'd think to myself "you know life is better than this . . . so why are you still here?"

To make matters worse, the people close to me couldn't understand the person I'd become. They still thought I'd just gone through a phase, a bit of rebellion, an extended vacation before settling down into the Matt I was supposed to be. They couldn't see that I was a new person.

And, when I started talking about leaving again, the reactions seemed to be the same.

I'd returned in one piece, but no one ever said to me, "Well, I guess you were right. The world isn't so dangerous, after all." Instead, they thought I dodged a bullet or got lucky.

My old coworkers still thought I was nuts. My friends were still indifferent, and my parents were still determined to convince me to stay home. Whenever I came down to breakfast in the morning, I'd find that my father had left job postings circled in red ink on the table. Everyone in my life was pushing me to stay put and go back to the way things always were, and always would be as far as they were concerned.

But the voice in my head—the one that said, *You know life can be better than this*—was still there. It told me, in a voice I knew was unmistakably the truth, that stopping my travels had been a mistake, and that the way to live a full life was to get back out there. No one could stop me. The more people told me "No," in fact, the more that voice screamed *Yes!*

Fortunately, I also learned a lot about what it takes to stick to a plan for your life in the face of skeptics, to pursue a dream even as the people around you incessantly question it—to constantly tell yourself *Yes* when the whole world is insisting on "No."

But, more importantly, having been through this once before, I knew what to do.

First, I found it helpful to transform all the negativity into positive energy—motivation to get out there and to prove them wrong. I'd tell myself: "I know they're wrong. I won't let them get me down. I'll only let them inspire me to do better." I've learned to enjoy proving people wrong. When someone tells me I can't do something, it pushes me to show them I can. That doesn't mean fixating on all of the "haters" in your life, making your travel plans to spite them. That's an ugly way to live, and it also means that you'll be going on someone else's trip—not your own. There's a difference between taking pleasure in spiting someone, and taking pleasure in exceeding expectations about yourself. The former is fixated on negativity, the latter is all about well-earned pride.

Second, I became proactive in finding encouragement. Just as before my first major trip, I devoured books, guides, and, now, blogs about destinations I'd daydream of visiting. I connected with fellow travelers and turned them into my support network. I asked a lot of questions. I did my homework. By reaching out to people who understood my wanderlust—even if it was just people I "knew" online, who had traveled and come back fine—I was able to overcome the negativity from those around me.

Like many people in a niche community, like many people who feel like outsiders or oddballs at home, the online community was a lifesaver. I didn't have to grow up in the same city, or even the same country, as people in the travel community to feel a deep connection with them. For all that we didn't share, the thing we did share—the passion for the open road—was the most important thing of all. Reaching out to them helped me feel less alone. They knew how I felt.

Third, I took refuge again in planning. I made a list of everything I needed to do for my next trip and I broke it down, step by step. By focusing on each small milestone, I could tune out the noise and stay focused on my goal. Getting to each next step on my personal plan was all that mattered to me. I'd learned a bit about planning since my earlier days as a nomad. I realized that plans themselves can and should change at a moment's notice—but more than ever, I knew that the planning process, a time when all the fantasies of your perfect trip come to life before your eyes, is something to be savored, not something to procrastinate or rush past.

No one I knew back home in Boston understood the pull of

constant travel. No one understood why staying still made me so bored, why it made everything feel so stale.

To most people, I had "done" my trip. Now it was time to stop being a weirdo and get with the system. It was time to start being smart and following the rules.

I don't blame them for that. They didn't have a frame of reference for that. To me, they were still stuck in *The Matrix* and, while that worked for them, it no longer worked for me.

They were genuinely worried because they couldn't fathom why the very clear risks—to career, stability, and my future—were worth more time on the road. They weren't aching to travel the way I was. All their reasons why I shouldn't go were all my reasons I should.

On the road, I felt as if I was living my life—my real life, the life I was meant to lead.

Many people travel the world to get the bug out of their system, or to check things off a list to say they've been there and done that. But the thing I have discovered about myself and other nomads like me: the more we travel, the more we want to keep traveling. You don't get the bug out of your system. Traveling only makes it grow. It's a disease with no cure.

Back home, I realized that there was still more to see of the world and more life to live. Being at home felt like I was dying—like a cage I'd claw my way out of if I could.

I'll admit that I'm the kind of person who, when faced with a tough situation, tends to retreat to his comfort zone. That was true in my awkward, nerdy youth, and it's still true now that I've become a nomad. What's changed—because everything changes—is my comfort zone. Now, travel itself is my comfort, the place I yearn to be when life is hard.

And, as I planned to go, I heard the same words from

people over and over again: I was running away. I heard it from my parents: I was running away from my home and my roots.

I heard it from my coworkers: I wasn't settling down and getting a conventional job, I was trying to run away from my problems.

It came from all quarters: When would I "settle down"? When would I "join the real world"? When would I "get serious"?

Commenters on my blog even joined in. One told me to stop running away and to get with the real world. If you ever spend time as a serious traveler, I guarantee that you'll hear some variation of this, too. I'm not sure why, but it seems to be conventional wisdom that anyone who travels long term, and isn't interested in settling down or getting a conventional job, *must* be running away from something. They are just trying to "escape life." Travel is fine, within limits—a short vacation, even a gap year before college or a backpacking and Eurail stint after. But talk seriously about a nomadic lifestyle, or linger just a bit too long, and you'll be sure to hear it: what are you running away from? Travel, the message goes, but not for too long and not too seriously.

We nomads must have awful, miserable lives back home. Or we're too strange to form lasting relationships. Or we're children who don't want to grow up, who desperately stay away from the real world.

As those words were constantly repeated to me, I finally realized that I had to stop fighting it. I stopped denying it. Yes, I told anyone who doubted me—you're right. I *am* running away. I'd been running away ever since I first slung my backpack over my shoulder in 2006. But I'm not trying to avoid life, I'd tell my doubters. I'm trying to avoid *your* life. I'm not running away from the real world—I'm running away from your idea of what the real world is.

Running away from office life, commuting, and weekend errands, and running toward everything the world has to offer. Running away from monotony, nine to five, rampant consumerism, and the conventional path.

I was running toward the world, toward exotic places, new people, different cultures, and my own idea of freedom and living. I wanted to experience every culture, see every mountain, eat weird food, attend crazy festivals, meet new people, and enjoy different holidays around the world.

I realized that casting deliberate vagabonds and nomads as crazy, maladjusted, antisocial Peter Pans is just another way of perpetuating fear. It's a way of saying "our life is the only life, and anyone who wants out of it is crazy." And when you define people who want out of your life as crazy, you never have to grapple with the shortcomings of your way of living.

The truth is that nearly all of us need someone to define ourselves against. Maybe you've heard this quote from the famous French poet Rimbaud: "I is another." What that means to me is that we all make up our own version of "I"—our notion of who we are as people, what makes us unique, what we value— by pushing off against someone else. None of us becomes an "I" without defining ourselves as something that another person is *not*. Other people help us to understand our own identity. If you sat around in a room all by yourself, for your whole life, you wouldn't know much, if anything, about the kind of person you were.

But we don't sit by ourselves in a room. We look at the siblings, parents, friends, enemies, and random strangers around us and figure out what makes up our "I." "I'm not athletic like him," you might say. "I'm better at drawing than that other kid." Or, "Most kids say they like chocolate ice cream, but I like straw-berry." Or, "I can't keep up in math class—maybe that's not what I'm good at."

Through hundreds of little little comparisons like this every day, we figure out who it is that we are. And as we get older, the comparisons get more comprehensive, and tend to harden. Re-sponsible, sedan-driving adults all across America are likely to tell themselves, *I'm not like one of those crazy people who picks up and moves all around the world. I've settled down and made a life here. It's not always glamorous, but at least I know who I am—and I'm not those people.* And, of course, nomads like me do the exact same thing in reverse. I know I have. I've told myself, "I'm not like all those sedan-driving normies who stay put their entire lives. I've ex-plored the world. It's not always easy, but at least I know who I am—and I'm not *those* people."

I've been especially prone to do this when the traveling is es-pecially hard—when someone snoring in the next bunk won't let me sleep, when my backpack straps dig into my shoulders, when I'm burned out from one too many bus rides or cold break-fasts. I have to admit that "I'm not *those* people" has kept me going through some hard times. *"It's still better than home,"* I'd say to console myself.

There's no getting out of this bind. We *all* define ourselves against other people—it's part of being human. No one can see what he looks like without looking at a reflection, and when it comes to our personalities and our values, other people are our reflection.

Making someone else your "other" is healthy, normal, nec-essary. But it can also become unhealthy. It can get way out of hand. And for me, where it gets out of hand most often is when you reach the point of treating others *only* as the points you define yourself against. You look at someone else—someone with a different story or a different path, a different personality or a different set of choices—and you don't see a fellow human being, you just see what you are not. You see a defective you, a freak. Some of us become so unconfident in our choices, so dependent on mentally running others down in order to make ourselves feel like we have worth, that we stop seeing other people as anything else but as a means to that end. At the extremes, this is where racism, sexism, and all the other bad-isms originate. But even when things don't get that extreme, it can mean diminishing other people before we've had the chance to understand them, just because they *aren't us*.

And so, just as I probably had an unfair image of the sedan-driving normie in my head, that guy had an image of a filthy, unwashed me in his head to help him get through his day. That's what Regular America does to mentally sustain a way of life that isn't all that healthy—set itself up in opposition to all of the hippies, nomads, weirdos, radicals, and freaks that it is not.

But I know how dishonest that move is, because I've met those "freaks." I've gotten to know nomads and vagabonds and people who don't fit in at home. I knew them firsthand. And they weren't antisocial weirdos: They were people with a lust and a zest for life, people who wanted to live it on their own terms, to soak up everything the world can offer. They were people who knew that life is short, and we only get to live it once. They were people who wanted to look back on their crazy adventures, not on their time at a desk, wishing they were somewhere else.

As for the people at a desk—well, they're not as awful as I'd imagined them, either. I had built an image in my head that came with youthful ignorance—and that age toned down. Some of my best friends have opted for the settled life, the life of minivans, suburbs, 2.5 kids, steady jobs, and 401(k) plans. That choice is right for them. And there's nothing wrong with choosing a rooted, settled life if you choose it consciously, deliberately.

So many of us do the opposite, though. We choose that life because it's the only option we see, or because we're scared out of considering alternatives, and then we spend the rest of our lives resenting our choice, because really it wasn't a choice at all. And, in a vicious cycle, we try to dull our resentment by casting those who opt out as crazy, as not-normals.

I wanted to run away from all of that. When Thoreau said that he wanted to "live deliberately," that resonated with me. He said that he wanted "to front only the essential facts of life, and see if I could not learn what it had to teach, and not, when I came to die, discover that I had not lived." That desire drove him to live in a cabin in the woods; it drove me to strap on a backpack and leave home. But I think the basic impulse is the same: to choose consciously, and not by default, how to spend the few years we're given.

Few people choose to live like that, and the people who do are always bound to generate some resentment from the people who don't. Conventions, rules, and molds are sacred to those who live by them, and they're likely to brand those who break them, people like me, with all of the hurtful words they can think of. And when people who live by conventions, rules, and molds find themselves dissatisfied, they'll make themselves feel better not by pulling up stakes, but by running down those who do, and wishing—just wishing—that their own lives offered something more.

Years ago there was a book called the *The Secret*. It was a bestseller, endorsed by Oprah herself. According to *The Secret*, if you just wish for and want for something bad enough, you'll get it. *Of course* that message was a bestseller, because everyone feels dissatisfaction from time to time, but most people aren't willing to do anything more strenuous than wishing it away.

But the idea that you can wish a rich and exciting life into being is ridiculous. The real secret to life is that you get what you want when you do what you want. Life is what you make it, not what you wish it. Life is yours to create.

We are all chained down by the burdens we place upon ourselves, whether they are bills, errands, or (in my case) blogging deadlines. When those burdens grow too heavy, we can choose to realize that almost all of them, on some level, are self-imposed—optional. Burdens are made to be thrown off. If you really want something, you have to go after it.

People who travel the world aren't running away from life. Just the opposite. Those who break the mold, explore the world, and live on their own terms are running toward living. We are running toward our idea of life. We get to be the captains of our ships. We looked around at what normal, "well-adjusted" life had to offer and said, "No thank you. I want something more, something different." Having seen the world, having seen there was another way to live, I couldn't go back.

That was the freedom and attitude I saw in the backpackers who first inspired me all those years ago, and that's why I left Boston again and embraced my place as a true nomad.

LIKE A DRUG, travel had kept its grip on me long after I thought I was done with it. And like an addict chasing their first high, it was never as good the second time around. So it was for my second trip around the world. I had gone back out to chase the high—imagining it to be a highlight reel and forgetting the ugly parts.

As I've said, we romanticize our trips. We remember those funny moments in hostels in Prague, on beaches in Thailand, and those nights laughing with pretty Spaniards in Florentine courtyards. We forget the long bus rides, the frustration at different cultures' views on time or safety, or those times you got sick—all those things that caused burnout in the first place. Those moments become funny anecdotes. Tales we swap around the bar.

That's the amazing thing about memory—it sands down the bad parts, the tedious parts, the frustrating parts, the burnout-inducing parts. And it works even when we know that that's what it's doing.

Back at home, in our old life, we think of all the happy memories of travel and contrast them with our boring day to day. We think of the moments we wish could last forever, and the places always seem to pull us back to them.

I've had those beautiful moments on that first eighteen month trip: my first stay in Amsterdam, living in Ko Lipe, Thailand, for a month, and lately, the island of Ios. In those moments, I found paradise. I found locations I still remember vividly in my mind and still pull me toward them no matter where I am in the world. I found people I connected with and who will stay with me for a lifetime.

Yet as I retraced the route of my original trip—first in Bangkok, then around Southeast Asia, then back again in Europe—I began to wonder if something was wrong with me. Because there was something missing the second time around. Something I couldn't put my finger on. As much as I wanted to run toward life, to get out there and explore again, the reality didn't seem to live up to my memories, or my anticipations. It wasn't as fulfilling.

I spent time living in Bangkok again, then moved to Taipei and worked on my blog, then went back to Europe, and in each instance my time settling down brought me more joy than my time traveling.

"It's simply chasing ghosts. Places will never be the same as they were. It's the people that make them. You are chasing the ghosts of travel past. That's why you're disappointed," Bill said to me.

Bill was a well-known travel writer. He had been in the industry for decades and I looked up to him greatly. I met him for drinks in New York City, where I had moved for the summer in 2010. I had always dreamed of having a wild summer in the city, and now with a job that gave me the flexibility to do it, I was.

Bill's point was that we can never get that back, because we can never get the people back. They are who matter—the places are incidental.

What really made Thailand so special? It was the people I met. Ko Lipe was magical because of John and Sophia.

We all try to chase ghosts. On an intellectual level, you know a place you visited years ago isn't going to be the same—you can't step in the same river twice. But on an emotional level, you still want to chase that high, even if you have to deceive yourself to get going. We all want to relive that high. Put ourselves back in that memory, with all of the bad parts edited out and only the shining parts left: new friends, lounging on beaches, exploring waterfalls on hikes, a delicious bowl of noodles or a late night out.

Whenever I meet people from those times, we relive those memories together. We reminisce about the beautiful and sometimes life-changing moments we shared. We talk about going back to those places and trying to recapture those moments. But what we really want to recapture is a spot in time, not a set of coordinates on the map. And there's no going back in time—there's only doing what we can to make new memories.

In many ways, Bill was right. You can never relive your best memories, because the people, the situations, the environment will never be the same. Trying so hard to recapture the past only makes it worse—it slips out of your grasp the harder you try to hold on, leading to bitter disappointment.

But I was never good at following people's advice. And, ignoring Bill's counsel, I went back to the place that spurred our conversation: Ios.

The Greek island of Ios is a rocky plot of land with a main town growing like a vine up a pointy, church-topped hill with quintessential blue and white houses, small cobblestones lanes, and tiny storefronts. The island's wide, yellow sand beaches are lapped by beckoning azure blue water. Small clusters of houses and terraced cliffs for wine and crops branch out from the main town. The island as a whole is a haven for young backpackers seeking to soak up the sun and to party.

My first time there, in 2010, had burrowed deep into my memory. Arriving in May that year, before the crowds, I found most of the other backpackers there were looking for work. Ios' economy in the summer runs on backpackers working the bars and restaurants in exchange for free food, drink, and enough money for a room.

As the days and nights ticked by, I developed a tight circle of friends. There was James, the suave ladies' man from Canada who was using his Greek passport to stay in Europe as long as possible. Mitch and Byron, who worked at one of the main bars and had come over from Australia together. Tim, another Australian who ran the beach water sports rentals, spending his fifth summer on Ios. Frances and Alice, two Scottish girls, escaping Scotland for the summer. Caitlin, a tall ginger from New Zealand with a sharp wit. These people became my core group of friends on the island. We were all travelers lured in by Ios' party reputation, beautiful weather, and stunning beaches.

Our days fell into a rhythm: we'd wake up late, hung over from the night before; head to the beach, eat lunch, relax, talk, and, at night, congregate on Tim and James's large roof deck for a BBQ. Each night, the gang would go over for dinner and a few drinks before they went to work. Occasionally, we'd invite other travelers to join our revelry. Later, we'd head out as a group for a bar and, one by one, my friends would drop like flies as they snuck off to work. Left alone, I would bounce between bars, hanging out with the backpackers who were passing through to binge heavily, or, unable to drink more after too many big nights in a row, simply head home to work on my blog and get some rest.

Most travelers stayed only a couple nights on Ios. They would party hard, sit on the beach, and, after a few days, stumble back onto the ferry, having checked Ios off their list. My friends and I were here for the long term—they because their travel plans depended on working and me because, having found a group of people I liked, saw no reason to leave. Staying put allowed us to create roots on a windy island where people blew in and out like leaves. Yes, there were other workers on the island, and I'm sure they formed their own cliques—but this one was ours. This was, at least temporarily, my family. Days and nights together, we chatted little about our life back home and the memories there, and we laughed about our shared experiences. We gossiped over hookups, bickered over where to eat that night, traded book suggestions, and sparred over the politics of the Greek economic crisis.

Now, trying to re-create that high, I found myself back on Ios in 2011. I was turning thirty and wanted to go to a place where I knew I could celebrate like I was turning twenty-one. I wanted a wild party, beautiful beaches, lots of travelers, and cheap alcohol.

That was Ios.

But, thinking about Bill's point, I arrived with a lot of trepidation. Was I just here to chase ghosts? Was I here for the destination or in hopes of refinding my tribe? Ios was another comfort zone. A place where I knew what to expect. A place where I felt I belonged. I could have spent time in a new place, but I knew I'd see familiar faces there, and that was what I wanted. I wouldn't be able to recapture those old memories of Ios, and that was fine, because I would still have some fun with the people with whom I shared those memories.

With no small amount of relief, when I arrived the locals remembered me and invited me back into their home like I was family. One night at the hostel bar, Francesco asked me if I had any plans. Francesco's hostel is an institution on Ios. It has been around for decades and, with its pool and close proximity to the bars, it is always sold out. During my extended time there the previous summer, I'd become close with Francesco and his wife, who found it curious that someone not working at the bars would choose to stay so long on the island.

"You have any meetings now for your blog or whatever it is?" he said.

"Nope, I was just going to talk to the people on the patio."

"Okay, I'm going to take you to a Greek festival at the monastery in the mountains."

"Right now?" I replied.

It was 10:00 at night. It seemed kind of late for a festival. But if there's one thing people learn quickly on Ios, it's that you never say no to Francesco. He has an imposing personality and is an important figure in the community. Francesco has the great ability to phrase a command as a question.

"Yes, right now. Come on, I'm driving."

We headed up the mountain. As Francesco quickly rounded every corner and veered along the tiny, winding mountain track in the dark, I shut my eyes. Francesco assured me we were fine, but I was always afraid we were going to tumble off the edge. In Greece, there are no guardrails.

"Don't worry! I've been on these roads all my life!" he assured me giving me a "fucking wimp" eye roll.

Arriving at the festival, Francesco ushered me into the back garden. In front of me were Greek women cleaning large food bowls while huge cooking pots heating soup and goat meat sat on top of large wood fires. Francesco grabbed me a clean bowl from the pile, poured some soup into it, and threw in some chunks of goat.

"Eat. It's like deer."

I sat down at a table full of Greek men who looked at me like I was an alien from Mars. Francesco said a few things in Greek, and the men smiled, making an eating gesture. They stared as I ate every bit of food. Here I was, a stranger in their world, and these old, cigarette-smoking Greek men watched me try whatever food I was given.

The goat was delicious. Tender, falling off the bone, it tasted a lot like lamb. I don't know what the soup was made of, but that, too, was good. It had a thick, rice-porridge consistency. The bread was airy and obviously homemade, soaking up the hot soup well.

After the soup came wine, more bread, and different cheeses—"from Ios" a grizzled man on the corner with a cap and long cigarette said. The soft goat cheese was some of the milkiest and smoothest goat cheese I've ever had. I cleaned the whole plate as a small Greek grandmother with a wooden cane and black shawl stopped and watched.

"Can I have some more?" I said cleaning the bowl.

This wasn't the kind of stuff they served to all us tourists back in town. This stuff was full of melt-in-your-mouth meat, crusty bread, and soup that was bursting with flavor.

After the meal and another glass of wine, I left the old patriarchs to go watch the dancing taking place in the front courtyard. As the band played on and the night got later, the crowd began to thin out. In the old days, they would have taken donkeys up to the monastery to stay the night. Now people stay until around midnight before driving back.

Francesco came and got me. It was time to go. "It's good. You like it?"

"Yeah, it was the most Greek thing I've done in Greece."

"Good. Write about it. It will make a better story than about you getting drunk with other backpackers. This is the real Greece. Not that other bullshit."

⊕

I'VE AVOIDED REVISITING a lot of places for fear that I'll "ruin" my initial experience there and walk away disappointed. For example, in my mind, Ko Lipe is a deserted island in Thailand where I made lifelong friends. Going back to a now-overdeveloped island teeming with tourists and resorts would be something I couldn't handle. It would be paradise lost.

But, as Francesco drove me back, I realized Bill and I were wrong.

You *can* return to a place and love it just as much—if not more—than the first time but only if you go back with different intentions.

If you go back expecting the same magic to happen, you're going to be disappointed. You can't play the same movie twice and if you're hoping for a rerun, you're just setting yourself up for failure. People are what really make a destination—a magical concurrence where time and place produced a magical cocktail of friends and experiences. All my favorite memories revolve around the people who were there and how they made me feel at the time. It was never the place. That was merely the backdrop.

Just as people who choose a conventional life can get tied down to jobs and mortgages, people like me who choose a nomadic life can get tied down by memories. We can become protective of them—so afraid of tarnishing them that we never again set foot in the place where those memories were made. But just as Bill had a point—you can't recapture what's gone—taking that advice too far can cause us to miss out on making new memories.

The problem wasn't with the place. It was me. It my false belief that a second visit could never recapture the first one. And while maybe it couldn't, it could be something new, and good in its own right. You can't relive the same moment twice, but you can still revisit a place you love. Going back doesn't have to mean chasing ghosts.

You have to go back because you love the food, or the weather, or the style, or the beaches, or the people. You have to go back for the sheer joy of it.

As I've spent over a decade on the road, I learned that chasing ghosts is just as bad as never giving a place a second chance. I hated Bangkok until I lived there. I hated Los Angeles until I had been there a handful of times. I didn't love Berlin until my second visit. So much of a place depends on such a wide variety of factors that it's hard to say a place is terrible based on just one visit. Likewise, there's no reason to resist going back because "what if it's not as good the second time around?"

Because I was too afraid of tarnishing my old memories, I almost missed out on the wonderful new memories I made on Ios. If I had decided to keep protecting my glass house, I would never have gotten to experience one of the most authentic, deeply enlightening moments I've ever had in my visits to Greece.

Since that awakening in Greece, I've found myself revisiting many places. But I no longer feel I'm chasing ghosts. Those first memories will always be special ones. I return now because I want to create new, deeper memories. Because I want to peel back the layers more.

Heraclitus—who was Greek, after all—would understand. While he told us that we couldn't step in the same river twice, he didn't tell us to stop stepping in rivers.

11

You Can Only "Run Away" for So Long

Adventure is a path. Real adventure—self-determined, self-motivated, often risky—forces you to have firsthand encounters with the world. The world the way it is, not the way you imagine it. Your body will collide with the earth and you will bear witness. In this way you will be compelled to grapple with the limitless kindness and bottomless cruelty of humankind—and perhaps realize that you yourself are capable of both. This will change you.

—MARK JENKINS

HOW WOULD YOU DESCRIBE your life? Could a few words encapsulate the highs, the lows, the joys, the sadness of it all?

When people ask me how I like travel, all I can reply is "Yes, I love it. It's great."

To explain all the highs, lows, joys, and frustrations would take hours of conversation. And even that would be futile. Those

who understand it don't need words, and for those who don't—
who haven't felt the pull of the road or woken up in a sweaty
hostel surrounded by foreign strangers—there will never be
enough words. The question asks for a short answer, the truth
requires experience.

Travel hits you with so many emotions it leaves you a bit
numb. You are constantly bombarded by new sights, smells, situations, and people that it takes time to process all that.

But the thing you forget as you navigate the sensory gauntlet
of the road is that someone else is traveling with you: time.

Suddenly, one day you wake up and ten years has passed.
You've aged out of dorm rooms. You relish your sleep. You don't
want to do that pub crawl, because hangovers don't linger
through lunch anymore, they camp out behind your eyes for
two days. You don't care to meet another twenty-three-year-old
traveler. You have more friends than you can keep track of
anyways.

Nobody tells you life changes. It just happens. Slowly and in-
sidiously.

Unlike the moment I went away, there was no defining moment over the last decade where I woke up and said "Yes, I'm
different now." It was an evolution. It was a process of incremen-
tally pushing myself, retreating to comfort zones, and pushing
myself again. Changes occurred imperceptibly, until finally
enough change accumulated that when I looked in the mirror
I saw a different animal.

One day, I found myself a travel writer. One day, I found myself walking up to a girl at a bar in Taipei with confidence. One
day, I found myself doing adventure sports I never would have
done before. One day, I was done. The constant push and pull
between fear and adventure, between the desire for the freedom

of the road and the need for financial security to stay there, had changed me.

It changed how I travel. I needed to slow down and, after my wake-up call with Heidi in 2011, I didn't want to travel as much. Life had become a Faustian bargain. Either I traveled or I worked and, when I did both, I found joy in neither. I wasn't giving both my twin loves (and yes, I really do love my work) the attention they deserved and as such, everything suffered. I would sightsee less, spend longer in each destination, but still take lots of days off, often in a row, in hopes of "fixing" this gnawing unhappiness in me. If that sounds a little like depression, well, I'm no doctor, but I'm also no fool.

I had built a career around being a nomad, and, though burnout was happening with increasing frequency, I couldn't seem to get off the road. I would go through the motions, because travel was who I was. My self-identity was tied up to the concept of me as a nomad. On the road, I felt like a king, and more and more it seemed, heavy was the head that wore the crown. Whereas before I could go months without feeling burnout, now it was only weeks before that happened.

This led to an internal crisis.

Travel was my thing. When I felt down or stale, I'd go away again and the cycle would repeat itself. Bored at home? Let's cash in miles and head to Iceland for a few weeks. Let's go sail the Caribbean. I'd tell the girls I'd date I wouldn't be gone long—maybe a few weeks. But then weeks would become months and they were gone by the time I came back.

I was a ship tossed around by gigantic waves. I had no direction. No course to follow. But, starting in 2012, I noticed life turned into a battle of disparate goals. I kept trying to live too many lives: traveler, business owner, New Yorker.

I was stressed. Juggling these different impulses had drained me. I didn't know how to do it anymore. The years had taken their toll.

Back in early 2012, I began to realize that, while I wasn't running away in the traditional sense, like a person on a treadmill, I wasn't getting where I was headed.

When the book was finally done and before I went to see Samantha in Bangkok, I took a trip to Bamboo Island, a small island in Cambodia that you can cross in ten minutes. There were only ten bungalows. No internet. No power except from 6:00 to 11:00 PM. No hot water. No fans. It's just you, the beach, a good book, and a handful of other people.

I went with two British friends who knew the manager of the resort, and he was having a "bungalow warming party" to celebrate a newly built bungalow. It would be him, the local staff, and us. On my last night there, I watched the travel movie, *A Map for Saturday*. As it ended and the travelers interviewed in the movie talked about going home and their sense of loss, I began to cry. No, crying doesn't describe it enough. I wept.

For the first time, I felt as if my travels were truly ending. Unlike before, I would be going home and there were no plans to come back.

I walked out of my bungalow and sat down on the beach.

Looking out at the ocean as tears ran down my face, I thought about the path that brought me to this beach in Cambodia. In the distance waves shimmered under the moon and stars. There was no breeze. Just another hot night in Cambodia. Even though the sun had set hours ago, the air hung heavy with humidity.

After six years on the road, I was going home to Boston. To apartment hunting, furniture shopping, cable bills, traffic, and making sure I have gas in my car. My future held book tours, conferences, work, and deadlines. Responsibility had crept back into my life.

Would I be able to pick up the routine after so long? Would it be like riding a bike? What a scary word. *Routine*. To me, it felt like death. The end of freedom, adventure, and the lifestyle I had come to know.

Behind me, I could hear travelers partying, laughing, and forging new memories. This was the end for me though, and the realness of it all evoked tears from me for the first time in years. Big, baby-like tears.

"Are you okay?"

I looked up to see a girl I didn't recognize standing over me. "Do you want to join us all for drinks? I think you're the only one not at the bar," she said in an accent that sounded a little Scandinavian.

"I'm heading home next week and just wanted a moment to myself. It's a hard thing to have to deal with, ya know? The end of all this," I said holding up my hands.

"Yeah, I would be sad, too. How long have you been traveling?"

"Six years."

"Holy shit! That *is* a long time! I'm eight months into a year-long trip. Six must have been amazing!"

"Yeah, it was," I said with a pause, ". . . the best part of my life."

"I can't imagine what it would be like to go back home after so long."

There was pity in her voice.

To a traveler, nothing is worse than the end where the fun stops and the pressures of society return. Whenever someone tells you they are heading home, you put your hand on their shoulder and say "I'm sorry" as if you're mourning the loss of a fallen comrade. You leave this adventure that seems to stretch on for eternity, a place where you are the captain of your own ship, for the rigid constraints of "the real world". The one we all tried so hard to stave off.

We sat in silence for a few minutes.

"Well, if you want to join us, you know where to go. Chris is going to play that chicken fried song again," she said as she stood up, her pity party coming to an end.

"Yeah, thanks. I just need a few more minutes," I said as she left. "I'll be there eventually."

⊕

MAYBE IT WOULDN'T BE SO BAD, not being permanently on the road. I might even become less stressed as I spend my days working in a self-made nine to five and then took breaks where I didn't have to work. I could make my own schedule. I'd take trips. Travel wasn't over.

That was the self-talk I practiced in my head as I flew home from Bangkok and then, looking for a city larger than Boston, moved to New York City, signed a lease, and bought a bed. I unpacked my bag, hung up my clothes, and filled my fridge with food.

As the book tour for *How to Travel the World On $50 a Day* ended in the spring of 2013, I took a few trips to Europe, sailed around the Virgin Islands, and went back to Southeast Asia for the winter. Slowing down proved harder than I thought. Whenever I felt bored or antsy, I'd simply find an excuse to leave the city. My empty fridge a testament to my transient nature.

As that year turned into 2014, I found myself living two lives: the life of a traveler and the life of a New Yorker. I moved in and out of the city often, justifying my travels not as travel but as "work trips" I needed to take to make sure the blog ran smoothly. I moved around. Fell in love again. Burned out again. My love/hate relationship with travel seemed to get worse the longer I went away. Or the more frequently. I couldn't tell.

Though I was living two lives during the years of 2013 and 2014, it wasn't until my friend Scott died in 2015 that I was living in a way that was keeping me from appreciating the benefits of either.

I can't remember when I met Scott Dinsmore but, like so many of my modern friendships, I know where: the internet. Scott ran *Live Your Legend,* a website about doing what you love. Over the years, we bonded over our shared love of travel, entrepreneurship, helping others, good cocktails, and Taylor Swift (we're both super fans).

Like me, Scott had a transformative travel experience. His came when he was turned down for a dream job and went instead to Spain to run with the bulls. A seven-week trip turned into a year, and Scott said that the experience changed how he looked at the world. "Spaniards prioritized enjoyment over money, and I realized life did not have to be lived the way it was in the States," he later wrote. "Exploring, seeking meaningful adventure and limit testing quickly became a huge part of life."

It was the same transformative experience that had shaped my own view of travel—it's no coincidence that Scott and I bonded. Later, shocked by discovering how many Americans report that they have fantasized about quitting their jobs, Scott founded a career-coaching company dedicated to helping people find challenging and fulfilling work. His TEDx talk on "How to Find Work You Love" was viewed nearly three million times. Scott's lessons from a life of exciting travel and fulfilling work resonated with so many people—and they certainly resonated with me.

We would often catch up at conferences. Our busy lives rarely overlapped but whenever I came to San Francisco, we'd meet up for breakfast. I was proud to call him a friend.

In early 2015, Scott and his wife Chelsea sold everything, slung their backpacks over their shoulders, and set off to travel the world. We chatted frequently as Scott peppered me with requests for advice and tips.

"Where do we go for nice weather? Are we crazy to go to Morocco in August? What's a great place in Central Europe to spend a month?"

I felt like his consigliere as he tried to conquer the world.

So when I woke up to the email letting me know Scott had died, I was in shock. There had been an accident. The details were fuzzy.

It turned out that Scott had died while climbing Mt. Kilimanjaro. It was the last day of his and Chelsea's trek to the top, and they were taking a trail that wasn't normally used. The trekking company had decided to use a different route not meant for beginners. There was a rock slide. Screams. No place to hide. Scott was hit by a falling boulder. It was over in seconds, and there was nothing anyone could do.

I always wonder what he was thinking in his last moments. When a rock is barreling down at you, what do you do? What did Scott do? Was he frozen in fear? Did he run the wrong way? Did he even know what was happening?

I read the email over again. I called my friends. I cried. I kept thinking it was going to be like the movies—the doctors would be wrong, he'd jolt back to life, and we'd all say, "You had us worried so much!"

But life isn't like the movies. Scott wasn't coming back.

Scott was always happy, talkative, and energetic. If you asked him how he was doing, he would almost always say he was at nine or ten. He had the unique ability to make people feel energized about even the most mundane things.

His death threw me for a loop. In Scott's last blog, he talked about his struggle to balance work with his desire to get off the grid. As he said, "I almost decided not to book this Tanzania trip because I didn't think I could (or should) step away. How ridiculous is that? To pass up an adventure I've talked about for years—because I'd convinced myself I couldn't disconnect. Or more truthfully, because I couldn't find the courage to do it."

I saw myself in Scott's words like I'd never seen myself before. He realized that always being connected created an unrealistic expectation for both himself and his community. That was exactly what I was doing. We *shouldn't* always be connected. Always being connected is not healthy or productive. No wonder I was constantly burning out. We need to sign off and interact with people in real life.

⊕

IN THE DAYS AFTER HIS DEATH, Scott's wife Chelsea told a reporter that he had truly disconnected from the distractions in his life. "He left us in one of the most beautiful places either of us have ever been. He was so happy. He was disconnected from everything other than nature and me." Scott's father said that "Scott lived more in his short thirty-three years than most do in a lifetime."

His loss was a tragedy—but it was also an end to a life well and deliberately lived.

Scott's passing made me question a lot of aspects of my life. What was I doing with my life? What was this all for? Scott lived his life in the most daring way possible, and he inspired people along the way. I was trying to do a version of that myself—but Scott's death reminded me that we can take none of our plans for granted. Just as soon as he started on his quest, he was gone.

If Scott had been alive, he'd tell me to stop delaying and take action.

This moment put into perspective a feeling I'd been struggling with for a while: you can't run away forever. As much as I hated to admit it, I was wrong, and everyone else was right. I *was* running. I *was* trying to have my cake and eat it, too and in the end, the thing I loved most—travel—had become an albatross that kept me from truly being the person I wanted to be.

So, inspired by Scott, I decided to finally take the trip I had been dreaming of for years: one final trip through Southeast Asia and South America. I wanted to try once more to get it out of my system, or at least to confirm that, whether I liked it or not, I was a nomad who was destined to always travel.

I needed to find out who I was. I needed one last big trip. I needed to know, to try to work on finding a balance, to come to terms with myself and what I really wanted. Travel had done that once before for me. Maybe it would do it again.

I needed a sign.

And I found one in the unlikeliest of places.

12

The Light

We find after years of struggle that we do not take a trip; a trip takes us.

—JOHN STEINBECK

LOVE REVISITED ME LIKE a long-lost friend in 2015. It was the kind of love that makes you question the direction of your life and gives you visions of families, minivans, and white picket fences.

I was in Laung Prabang, Laos. After the bars closed, all the backpackers went to the local bowling alley. Bars in Laos are supposed to close at midnight but, because corruption is rife, the town's bowling alley paid off the local officials to stay open. Since it was the only place open, it was the one place everyone went to.

I was at the bar ordering a drink when someone stepped up to the bar next to me.

"You're Nomadic Matt, right?"

"Yeah."

"I love your blog, man. I've used it many times on my trip," he said to me shaking my hand. "There's a girl in our group who also likes it, but she's too shy to say so. She was the one that spotted you, actually. Come say hi if you have a chance!"

I looked over to see a blonde-haired woman in the corner.

"Cool. I might. Thanks," I said grabbing my drink and heading back to my friends.

Back at my table, everyone around me was in an intense conversation. As I sipped my drink, uninvolved in any of the conversations, I grew bored. They were talking in languages I didn't understand and I wasn't motivated to interrupt them and ask them to speak English. I looked back at the guy and his friend, got up and walked over to them.

I said hello again to the guy from the bar and introduced myself to his friend.

"I'm Matt," I said.

"I know. I'm Charlotte," she replied.

I laughed. "Yeah, your friend said you knew me. I guess just force of habit, right?"

"Are you American? Where are you from?" I continued.

"Yeah, I'm from Chicago. It's funny seeing you at the bar in Laos. Small world," she said dragging out the last two words a bit awkwardly.

About five-foot-seven with long blonde hair and chestnut colored eyes, this girl with freckles and an awkward manner was captivating. I don't know if love at first sight exists, but the moment I met her came as close as I had ever come to believing in it. I couldn't take my eyes off her.

We spent the night talking to each other, diving deep into our travels, how we ended up in Laos, how she ended up quitting her job, her previous life working and living in New York

City, my recent summer living there, our likes and dislikes. The conversation flowed like the bowling alley beer we knocked back.

When the night ended, and everyone headed back to town and said their good-byes at the town square, we lingered awkwardly.

"Let's go visit some of the temples and wander around the city tomorrow," I said.

"Sure, that sounds fun," she replied.

"How about 9:00 AM? That's not too early, is it?"

"No, it's fine. I haven't done much sightseeing yet, so that will be good. You can help me with filming a video."

"Sure! No problem," I said with a smile.

There was an awkward silence between us. The kind of silence where you wonder if you are supposed to go in for a kiss or just say goodnight.

Fuck it, I thought. I went in for the kiss.

She kissed me back and then took a step away.

"Wow, that was unexpected," she said. "But not that bad."

She smiled.

I kissed her again and we walked back to her guest house.

"I'll see you in the morning. 9:00 AM, right?"

"Yes, I'll meet you here!"

I leaned in again and we kissed passionately for what seemed an eternity. Breaking away eventually, Charlotte said goodnight, went into her guesthouse, and I skipped home to bed where, unfortunately, I didn't manage to get much sleep.

In the middle of the night, I awoke with a sharp pain in my stomach. I looked at the clock. It was 3:00 AM. I bet it was those chicken skewers I had earlier. I knew they tasted funny. As dawn broke, and the crippling certainty of food poisoning worked its way through and out of my exhausted body, all I could think of was that I had no way to contact Charlotte to tell her that I was basically dying from street food. But there was no way I was going to stand her up. Who knows where this could lead, but it would go absolutely nowhere if I didn't show up and didn't say why. So I rose from bed and took a shower. Chugging a bottle of water, I combed my hair, shaved, and put on clean clothes, trying to make it appear I was healthy and rested.

It took me some time to find Charlotte's guesthouse. It was in an alley off the main street that looked very different in daylight. Once I found it, I went inside and looked around. Charlotte wasn't there. There were a still a few minutes before nine. The check-in lady gave me weird looks as I stood there so I went back outside and waited.

"Sorry I'm late. I'm pretty hungover and I woke up late," she said coming out the door a few minutes past nine.

"It's okay. I'm not feeling too well either," I said as we hugged hello.

We walked to the main town square and had smoothies from the stands that were a staple of every traveler's diet here. They were cheap, healthy, delicious. Everything you needed.

We sat at one of the plastic tables in front of the stalls, and got lost once again in conversation. Before we knew it, over an hour had passed. Realizing the time, we got up to sightsee and walked to a nearby temple, Wat Mai. Located on the main street, it was a multitiered temple with a fire-red roof accented in gold, dating back to 1780.

We were walking around the temple's large courtyard when it happened.

"Uhhhh, Charlotte, I think I am going to be sick. Hold this," I said handing her the rest of my smoothie. "I'm really sorry . . .

just . . . just . . . I'll be right back," I said, trying to run out of the temple grounds.

I didn't make it ten feet before I keeled over and vomited my smoothie onto the temple courtyard. I'm pretty sure this was not the kind of sacrificial offering a Laotian Buddhist temple is built to accept, so I scurried out to the street and continued to throw up. I took out a napkin from my bag, cleaned off, and then went to a nearby bathroom to wash up. Composing myself, I walked back to Charlotte who stood there dumbfounded.

"Sooooo sorry about that. I think I ate something bad last night," I said as my cheeks flushed red. "I am really sorry. This is the most embarrassing thing ever."

She handed me back my smoothie.

"Do you want to go home?"

"No, it's okay. I feel a lot better now. I just shouldn't have forced this heavy smoothie into my stomach," I said. "I thought it would help. I was up all night sick. I think it was dinner, 'cause it wasn't the 'I drank too much' kind of sick."

"Why did you come out if you weren't feeling well?"

"Well, I had no way to reach you. I didn't want you to think I was some sleaze who cancelled because we didn't hook up last night. And I didn't want you to think I just made plans so I could hook up with you either. I actually really wanted to hang out with you today."

She laughed.

"I probably would have thought that."

"Should we get out of here before anyone notices I just threw up? It's probably super sacrilegious."

"Yeah. That's probably a good idea."

We smiled at each other and walked out of the temple. I grabbed some water from a vendor to rinse the taste of sick from my mouth and begin to replenish my fluids so I could make it through the rest of our stops: first, the palace, which was now a memorial and history museum about the days when the country had a king; then climbing Mount Phousi, a large hill in the center of town, to the temple, Wat Chom Si, on top where you got sweeping views of the city, the river, and the far-off jungle.

After Wat Chom Si, we ate a simple lunch of soup—that was about all my stomach could handle at that point—and headed to my guesthouse, where I brushed my teeth and grabbed my bags. I was transferring to a hotel by the river, because the current place I was in was fully booked. The new hotel was a beautiful building with teak rooms, a balcony, a bathroom, air-conditioning, and TV. It might not have been much to anyone else but, to a backpacker who spends most of their time in $5 a night dorms, this opulent $20 a night hotel was a palace. Stepping into my room, I could see Charlotte's eyes widen and I knew she was thinking the same thing I was: *I could get used to this!*

The following day we went to see the Buddha caves. Getting in a long-tail boat near town, we took a tour up the Mekong River to Pak Ou, where over four thousand Buddha statues are located in a series of caves on the river. These caves are important shrines to the local people and we saw many locals burnings incense and offer prayers. With the two hours upstream from Luang Prabang, it was a relaxing day taking pictures on the river and enjoying the sounds of the jungle as we came back.

"Why don't you come stay with me? It will save you some money on your room." I asked as we drank beers and watched the sun set over the river.

"I dunno," she said.

It had only been two full days and nights but travel speeds

relationships up and with no plans to stop seeing her, it made sense to me. However, Charlotte told me she was still hurting from her previous relationship—one that helped spur this trip— and wasn't quite ready to make that kind of emotional leap yet. They had been together for a decade—her one serious boyfriend—and he had cheated on her.

"Well, it's up to you. I already booked the place."

The next morning as we laid in my bed, Charlotte looked at me with an awkward, coy smile and said, "Shit, I forgot to ex- tend my last place. I'll have to move in with you, I guess. Hope- fully it won't be weird!"

"Charlotte," I said with a laugh, "we're always weird together. That's why we get along!"

She laughed in agreement.

What was supposed to be a few days in Luang Prabang be- came a week. There isn't much to do in the area once you've seen all the temples and gone up river, but with the cafés, beau- tiful sunsets, and sleep-inducing hangovers, it's easy to find your- self stuck there for longer than anticipated.

And, as Charlotte and I both had online jobs, we had plenty to do during the day to occupy our time. We would wake up, eat a delicious breakfast, head to a funky café to work, wander the city, take a nap, and relax. We revisited temples, waterfalls, and bars.

But, eventually, we had to say good-bye. She was going toward Chiang Mai for Loi Krathong, where Thais celebrate the lunar new year and send thousands of lanterns into the air for good luck. I was going to keep exploring Laos with some friends who had come to visit me.

After she left, we stayed in constant contact. Every day was bookended with a call or FB chat. We made plans to meet back up in Bangkok. I rented an Airbnb and met Charlotte at the airport. I was ecstatic. I couldn't believe it. She was here in real life. She hadn't found a reason to leave. I hadn't found a reason to run. For the first time in a long time, someone liked me as much as I liked them, and I hadn't screwed it up by either being too needy or too rooted to my work.

Charlotte was everything I wanted in a woman. I'd found pieces of her in the other women I dated or hooked up with, but the fact that they were never all in one package was one of the ways I explained to myself why I'd been single for such a long time.

The truth, though, was that I never really wanted a girlfriend. I loved the *idea* of a girlfriend—someone to explore with, someone to love me, someone to love back, someone to be a constant in a lifestyle that always fostered change—but in reality, Samantha rightly guessed I wasn't ready to commit to a long-term relationship. Travel was my first love. I wasn't ready to get tied down. I wasn't ready to commit to something serious and long term. Travel made it easy to avoid commitment. It let me never get too close or emotionally vulnerable.

But, now in Bangkok, with Charlotte sitting next to me, I felt ready to finally take the leap.

⊕

LOVE ALWAYS SEEMS TO HAPPEN when you least expect it. I wasn't looking for love on this trip. I simply wanted to come to peace with myself and what I wanted out of my life.

I found that peace in Charlotte. She showed me that I wanted to settle down. That I was finally ready. In her eyes, I saw a future.

We stayed together for the remainder of her time in Thailand before she flew to Australia. She was doing a working holiday and joining the ranks of the thousands of backpackers who go to Australia each year to work and earn money for travel.

When she left that fateful December morning, I was as depressed as I had even been over a girl. Though I didn't tell her then for fear of pushing her away, I knew I was in love. I couldn't remember ever having really loved someone like this, and seeing her walk away crushed me.

After she left, I needed to get my mind off of her, so I headed to a destination that had long been on my list: Isaan. I had never been able to get to there, despite over a decade of coming to Thailand. My original plans fell through as I became a teacher and, every subsequent visit to Thailand always seemed to pull me elsewhere.

Thailand's Isaan region was still one of the most under-visited parts of the country. Travelers simply pass through it on their way to Laos, or skip it altogether in favor of places like Pai, Chiang Mai, or the islands of the south.

All of which was fine by me.

Isaan—a land of mostly farms and villages, architecturally uninspiring cities, and spicy and delicious food (some of the best in Thailand)—is one of those places where you can get off the trail and see what life, unspoiled by tourists, is really like in Thailand.

I took scenic bike rides through the rice fields, farms, and small towns, and down dirt roads. I visited ancient Khmer temples where I was the only Westerner, with groups of Thai kids giving me funny looks. I visited national parks and dusty villages with incredible local markets, and was taken to play badminton by local teachers I met while eating in Ubon Rat-chathani.

It was marvelous, but it wasn't the same without Charlotte. I wanted to share the fun and joy with her and I counted down the days until I'd see her again.

We continued to talk every day. I would retreat back to my hostel to work and talk to her. We'd talk about our days, laugh at each other's jokes, discuss the news, and spend hours just day-dreaming about life. It always felt as if she was in the bed next to me.

I had our whole future mapped out. I'd meet her for New Year's in Bali, go back home to speak at the *New York Times* travel show, then visit South America before heading to Australia and New Zealand with her. In June, when her brother got married, she'd come back and we'd hang out in the States, she'd be my date to my roommate's wedding, and then we'd just keep traveling and live happily ever after.

When we met up in Bali for the new year, it was like we had never been apart. Our days filled up with magical dinners, sailing trips, time on the beach, and nights in each other's arms. On our last night, as we ate room service and listened to jazz in bathrobes at our hotel, we looked into each other's eyes in bed.

"I love you, Charlotte."

"I love you, too, Matt."

For the first time in years, I had said those fateful words, meant every one of them, and someone said them back.

⊕

"DON'T COME HERE," Charlotte said. "It's super boring. You'd hate it. Go to South America and then we will meet up after." Charlotte would tell me this repeatedly while I was back home, preparing to leave for South America but thinking of just going straight to Australia to see her instead.

"I want to see you but all I do is work and you'll be bored." She was right. She was still working in the same small town in Australia whose only attraction, as far as I was concerned, was her.

Plus, I'd always wanted to visit Argentina. It was a land of food, wine, and stunning lakes, glaciers, and mountains. It was the birthplace of Evita. A mix of European and South American culture. Buenos Aires was supposed to be the Paris of South America. Everyone raved about it, and somehow, in eight years of travel, I'd never managed to get myself down there. I couldn't pass this trip up, so I relented in my romanticism, and got on a plane headed south southeast instead west southwest.

Buenos Aires was everything everyone said it would be . . . for exactly two days. Then my brain broke.

Here's the thing about trying to escape: Your feelings come with you. They sew themselves into the nooks and crannies of your backpack and hang there like dead weight, digging into your shoulders as you carry them from one beautiful place to the next. On this trip, I wasn't just dogged by the sadness of being without Charlotte, I was under immense pressure from all the work that had accumulated as NomadicMatt.com grew into a site with a million monthly visitors. There were the simple demands for more content and user experience improvements, but as I began to monetize the site with a branded store and courses on how to travel, there was also a massive amount of busy, technical work that was about as far from traveling—or even writing about travel—as the owner of a travel website could get. No matter what I did, everything else suffered and I fell deeper into a hole.

Over the preceding year, and with growing rapidity, I had begun to suffer from anxiety from constantly overworking myself. I felt that I could no longer balance my twin desires to settle down and travel. My eye began to twitch, I became restless when I sat down to work, and I needed to take Ambien to fall sleep.

In Buenos Aires, I was writing speeches for a few talks I had agreed to give, finishing a set of ebooks, talking to Charlotte at odd times since I was fourteen hours ahead, writing my blog posts. But the whole time I felt extremely guilty (or maybe it was shame?) about locking myself up in a hostel and working while in a destination I had so longed to just explore.

This wasn't why I wanted to travel. The threads of the two lives I had been leading started to pull away from each other. No matter which one I chose any given day—sightseeing or work—I felt guilty about not choosing the other.

I snapped. I started taking Xanax to calm down. I sank into a depression.

Something had to give.

I needed a place where I could see nothing and do work. I wanted to clear my plate so I could start fresh. I figured if I could just sit in one place, go through my to-do list, cancel some projects, and hit the reset button, I could solve my problem and get rid of my anxiety.

I decided to go to Mendoza. It seemed like the perfect place to relax. There wasn't much to do and, with a friend coming to visit before we went to Patagonia, I *couldn't* visit anything as I had to wait for her. I rented an Airbnb, locked myself in, and dove into my work. I caught up on all outstanding issues, nuked my unread email, and just said "enough."

But I was putting a Band-Aid over a deep wound.

On my third night there, I had my first panic attack. Sitting at my computer in my Airbnb, I suddenly felt like I couldn't breathe. My arm went numb. My chest hurt. It felt like a heart attack combined with an unending sense of doom.

I called my mom. She was a nurse.

"Was I having a heart attack?"

"If you were, you'd be dead already. But you need to call a doctor. I told you I was worried about you. You work too much. Why don't you come home?"

"No, no, I can't. I just need to do this. I'll call a doctor."

"Please be careful. Stop working! See a doctor. Relax. Call me soon!"

"I have some Xanax. I'll take that."

The Xanax calmed me down, if only temporarily. A panic attack is like drowning. It feels like you are suffocating but don't know why. There's a feeling of hopelessness that comes with it. And despair. Unending despair. The weight of the world is pushing on your chest, collapsing your lungs. It breaks not just your body but your spirit. Everything begins to feel like it's too much to handle.

Your heart and chest tighten, you feel light headed and scared. At least I did. I felt scared. Like nothing was enough and I was never going to be enough.

As I thought about the causes of my anxiety, I kept coming back to the word *have*. I have to do this, I have to write this thing, I have to visit this place, I have to attend this event, I have to go to this meeting, I have to say yes to this.

I fell into "the busy trap" where we say yes to everything. Suddenly, we get caught up in a cycle and we're going nonstop. We're overcommitted, burnt out, and drinking energy drinks or coffee just to stay awake. But we can't see a way out. I always thought this was something that happened to other people. People with a routine and office jobs. Now, I realized I was wrong. I was overcommitted and trapped in my own way.

My panic attack was a wakeup call.

I didn't need to say yes to everything or everyone. We are the masters of our ship, and if we don't want to do something, we don't have to! It wasn't until my eye started twitching and my chest tightened that I began to really understand this view.

By the time my friend came to visit, I felt more in control. The Xanax was helping and focusing solely on one thing helped focus my mind. I worked, read, worked some more. I cooked dinner, and then worked. The less work there was, the calmer I felt.

On one of our first excursions, we went to a little town south of Mendoza called San Rafael where you can take wine tours and follow bike trails on trips though the valley. We hiked all over and stayed up talking to the travelers in our hostel. It felt like what I remembered the nomad's life could be. The next day we moved to a hostel in a different town.

That night as I typed away on my computer, three Argentinian guys on vacation from Buenos Aires invited us to drink wine with some of the other hostel guests and staff in the backyard. My friend said yes but I declined because I wanted to finish some work.

"Did you come to Argentina to work or did you come here to drink wine and have fun?" they said, prodding me the way only people who, as Scott Dinsmore put it, prioritized enjoyment over money could.

I politely declined again but I couldn't stop thinking about their question.

It hit me like a punch in the gut. It was like someone had thrown a medicine ball at me while I wasn't looking.

They were undeniably right. I didn't travel to work. I didn't travel to sit behind a computer. I could do that from home. I had fallen into the same trap that kept me from sailing the San Blas Islands with Heidi all those years before. I wasn't leading a balanced life and it was because of that that I had developed such bad anxiety.

Here I was in a place I had dreamed of visiting for years, only to have spent most of my time working behind a computer in a vain attempt to finish a never-ending to-do list. Moreover, being in a new place and not enjoying it only *added* to my anxiety and disappointment. If I was going to travel to only work, what was the point of traveling in the first place?

I was a failure. I had let a workaholic tendency take control of my life. Those guys were right. In a moment of clarity, I closed my computer, put it in my room, and went outside to join them. There, we drank endless bottles of wine, ordered late-night pizza, and discussed the cultures and customs of our countries until the wee hours of the night. We laughed, we cried, we became friends.

Work was not why I had left my home all those years ago. My goal was not to work from anywhere. My goal was this. To get to know new people in new places. To peel back the onion and see how the world ticked. I went to sleep that night happier and more content than I had been in a long time.

With a killer hangover and a large cup of coffee, I sat down in the common area, opened my computer, and a pang of guilt swept over me. The pain in my chest resurfaced as I looked at my email and realized all the work I had left to do.

"I should have worked last night. I could have gotten a few more hours in. When I am in Patagonia, I won't have any internet access. I need to do this," I said to myself. I was mad at myself for having fun.

I began to redo my to-do list.

Then their question came back to me like a bad dream.

"Did I come here to work or did I come here to drink wine?"

Being in Mendoza didn't fix my anxiety, because I never fixed the underlying causes of it. I was working through the symptoms—my to-do list—but that would just get replaced by another list when it was done and the cycle would repeat itself.

Sometimes the best way to defeat an enemy is to deny it battle. I was *fighting* against the never-ending tide of my to-do list. I could work until the end of time but that wouldn't have changed anything.

My priorities were out of whack. I couldn't work and travel any longer. I saw that.

The world would not end if I didn't publish a blog post.

I was not going to let work win.

That would have just made everything for naught. To travel to escape the nine to five only to shackle myself virtually to a desk and end up in the same place.

I had lost my freedom and it was time to get it back.

I cancelled the talks I was supposed to give. I deleted all my emails, and put up an out of office message that explained my anxiety, how I was taking a break, and that no email would be responded to. I gave my assistant instructions to ignore emails, focus on a few projects while I was away, and not to bother me unless something major happened. I decided to continue to write, because it was cathartic for me, but all other projects would stop.

I would not find Argentina from behind a computer screen.
I had hit rock bottom.

It was time to take control of the situation and make radical changes.

⊕

ANXIETY DOESN'T VANISH at the flick of your fingers. It was a miracle that I made it to Patagonia with my friend, and I was proud of myself for making the right choice and getting down there instead of down to the bottom of my to-do list, but I was still struggling with my anxiety and what to do about it. It takes time to undo bad habits. It takes time to heal. And it's not always clear where the best place is to spend that time.

Was it Patagonia? We'd been there on an organized hiking tour for a week already, our last nights, in legendary Torres del Paine, were coming up, and I still wasn't sure.

Argentina's most popular park, Torres del Paine was founded in 1959. It is home to tons of glaciers, glacial lakes, deep valleys, famous granite mountains, and beautiful pine forests. More than 100,000 people visit each year, making it one of the top destinations in South America.

As we approached the park, giant gray mountains rose high above us and a cloudless blue sky stretched to infinity. Everyone on the bus gave a collective gasp. While our guides stopped to get our camping and hiking permits, we piled out for photographs. The crisp air, grass waving in the wind, and sheer mountainsides made me excited to get connected to nature again.

The paved road became dirt, and the bus—lacking any shocks—jostled us like a carnival ride. Over two days, we hiked the famous W trek, first to Glacier Grey, so named for the coloring produced by dirt as it collects in the glacier, then through the French Valley, where we ascended through burned forest, rivers, and along a valley, before arriving at Francés Glacier. There, melting ice came crashing off cliffs like intense thunder. We stood in the glacier's shadow, eating lunch and waiting for the cracking ice.

On the last day, we set out to tackle the park's most famous hike: the twenty-two-kilometer round-trip to the Torres Towers, one of the most difficult I'd done since the twenty-kilometer Tongariro Crossing in New Zealand. But these three towers set on a glacial lake are picture perfect, with their granite, ice-covered spires set above an aquamarine lake, and worth any hike. I could swear it was a photo used as computer wallpaper.

After my group ascended to the top, ate lunch, and started back, I opted to stay behind. I wasn't ready to leave. I found the area too peaceful. Staring at the Torres peaks, the energy of the area calmed me down and for the first time in a long time, I was content to just be. To just enjoy where I was without worry of what work was waiting for me at the bottom of the mountain.

Over the previous few days, I had thought about work a lot. It loomed in the back of my mind as the days ticked by and I wondered what was going on in the outside world. Was everything okay? But I realized, if something had gone wrong, there was nothing I could do anyway, so why freak out? Here in front of this natural wonder, worry faded from my mind.

I couldn't change the things I had no control over. I had to learn to let go. The cause of my anxiety was that I had overextended myself. If I wanted to get rid of my anxiety, I would have to change my life.

Patagonia is one of those locations on earth that makes you realize how small you are and just how grand and significant nature is. When I came back to civilization, I found that nothing had changed. My website didn't go down. The sky never fell. No one cared that I wasn't answering emails. In fact, the opposite was true. Most people were happy I was taking a mental health break and encouraged me to not get so wrapped up in work.

It felt odd. Here I was exposing a life of freedom and flexibility to millions of hopeful nomads, while I was slowing wrapping myself up in chains and doing the opposite.

As I boarded a flight to Australia at the end of February 2016, the month I had spent offline flooded back to me in a rush of reflection. I had found the cause of my anxiety and I had learned that being offline wasn't the end of the world. There were still flashes of worry. Flashes of panic. Something that takes control of you for so long doesn't go away so easily, but the month-long detox had at least put me on the road to recovery.

I found the cause of my discontent.

Now it was time to find that solution.

It was a solution that would teach me my most valuable lesson yet—and forever change my relationship with Charlotte.

13

Home

TEN YEARS. That's how long I spent on the road. To say that travel consumed my identity would be fair. To millions, I wasn't Matthew Kepnes—I was Nomadic Matt. To them, I am the guy without a home (or a last name), the blogger, the professional traveler. I don't recoil from that. I love it.

My original plan to travel the world, get traveling out of my system, and find a real job never panned out. One day bled into the next until, in the blink of an eye, a decade passed.

The Southern writer John Graves wrote only two books: One, *Goodbye to a River*, is a classic travel memoir about a trip to see the Brazos River before it disappeared behind modern dams and lakes—it was an ode to man's refusal to settle down or be in one place. Later in life, he wrote *Hard Scrabble*, which was in almost every way the opposite book—about his journey to carve out a home in the Texas Hill Country. It's about what he calls "The Syndrome": our need to own a piece of earth and our refusal to leave it once we do. He has a quote that I think encapsulates the tension and uneasy balance between these parts of ourselves:

> The provincial who cultivates only his roots is in peril,
>   potato-like, of
> becoming more root than plant. The man who cuts his
>   away and denies
> that they were ever connected with him withers into
>   half a man.

I looked back on the last ten years of my life—the wanderlust, the burnout, the oscillation between the urge to leave and the pull to stay—and realized that the tension, the anxiety, wasn't inside me, rather it *was* me. It was the result of a life lived out of hundreds of thousands of miles and countless nights in cities I don't fully remember.

I had fallen into travel writing. It seemed like a good way to keep traveling and, as my website grew, I continued to work on it without any real plan. I enjoyed it, and it kept me traveling, so it wasn't all bad.

But, as time wore on, I struggled with a secret, one I kept inside for fear of losing what had become my identity. The thing I craved most of all—more than anything in the world, no matter where I was at any point during that decade—was a garden. I had stood on mountaintops with soaring views, been awed by ancient temples, seen oceans that stretched to the furthest horizons, and traded stories in seven different languages before the day was out—but the thing I wanted to do most of all was come home to *a fucking garden.*

That garden became my next version of the guidebook I bought all those years back in 2005. It was the manifestation of desires for a next step.

A garden requires constant attention. Attention that can't be given when one leaves every few days. To have a garden would require me to settle down. A garden would be an act of commitment. A hobby that required myself to be rooted next to my rooted plants. To take them inside and turn them into a meal. In my own kitchen with all the tools never found in a hostel kitchen.

The garden became my proxy for settling down.

I would tell my friends how my next trip would be the last. Then they would see me jet off to this Southeast Asian country or that European city. And, when I'd come back, I'd promise that no, THIS one would be the last one.

"We're sick of hearing how you're going to settle down," they would retort. "It's a lie."

"No, I swear this time I really mean it. *This* is my last trip."

But they were always right. It *was* a lie. I was trying to have it all.

I understood now why alcoholics in a 12-step program give themselves over to a higher power: It's because you need something big and powerful in your corner when you're fighting an addiction. You need something to surrender to, someone to hand the wheel over to.

When I wasn't traveling, I was living New York City in an attempt to settle down in the most cosmopolitan place I could think of. I hadn't even been in my first apartment for two weeks before I bought a cheap flight and hit the road again to Europe and then the Caribbean. I'd just concocted this whole lifestyle plan so I wouldn't land myself in trouble with anxiety or burnout, and here I was back on the road. That was my life: I'd get back, get the itch, and scratch it.

Here's the problem: Because of my online presence, leaving wasn't that hard to do. The chorus egged me on, and when you're getting praise and jealousy for setting off to exotic locations, it isn't that hard to buy a ticket and throw a few clothes in a backpack. Then you get there, you have your fun . . . and then you come back to the same empty apartment and the same persistent questions about the new (bad) habits you've built.

Except I just couldn't do it anymore. The writer Mary Anne Radmacher once wrote: "I am not the same, having seen the moon shine on the other side of the world." I wasn't the same guy who was coached by some backpackers in Thailand to cast out and set off for the unknown. I had a deeper sense of who I was, *because* I had seen the moon shine on the other side of the world.

I couldn't let go of that self.

I knew that my longings for family and a relationship and some stability weren't just stray thoughts that popped into my head. They were real things I wanted. I was ready for them.

I was trying to beat these thoughts back and tune them out.

If I go away on one more trip, they will go away.

But your demons and desires travel with you.

And I could no longer ignore them.

⊕

WHEN CHARLOTTE ARRIVED IN MY LIFE, I realized that for the first time I had found someone to settle down with. I had found the companion I always wanted. The nerd, the politico, the traveler, the artist, the person who made me laugh, challenged me, and made me feel loved.

When I landed in Australia, she greeted me at the airport. She held up a little sign and surprised me with a card. She knew I had always wanted that. We smiled and kissed each other. On the bus ride back into town, we stared at each other and smiled. It was if we had never been apart.

We settled into our Airbnb in downtown Melbourne, which we planned to use as our base before traveling on to New Zealand together. It was a luxurious one-bedroom with hardwood floors, walk-in closets, a king bed, and a giant kitchen.

After a few days though, our honeymoon ended.

You learn a lot about a person when you travel with them. Forced into a compressed ever-changing environment, you learn how they deal with change and stress, overcome challenges, and interact with people. You learn if your lifestyles line up.

But you learn even more when you leave the travel bubble and live with them in "the real world." In a shared space, it's not lifestyle you learn about, it's personal idiosyncrasies. Do they squeeze the toothpaste tube from the bottom or the top? Do they replace the toilet paper roll so that it unspools from the top or from underneath? Do they leave lights on, do they leave laundry everywhere? Toilet seat up or down? Sleep with the heat on or the heat off? Air-conditioning at 67 or 71? Will you still have the same fun with that person you met on safari when you're dealing with questions like these? With commutes, bills, and whose turn it is to clean the dishes? When you don't have things to do 24/7, when you have to go to work, do laundry, go grocery shopping, will you still get along?

For Charlotte and me, it wasn't a sure thing. The real world was proving harder than we thought, and it turned out we didn't know as much about each other as we thought we did.

We decided we would each plan a day for the other. She loved libraries and cafés, so I booked her a tour of the library and walking tour of famous cafés. She booked a trip to see penguins knowing I love, well, anything. We both hated each other's day. She hated walking tours. I hated long bus rides. Little comments about how long a walk was or how inconvenient the weather was, were seen as personal slights and criticisms of the other person's decisions. It turned out I had work but she didn't, so my work days left her feeling stuck and stranded.

We began to fight about our expectations and our desires.

My panic attacks revealed the nature of the stress my dual life was causing, I realized something else: I *wanted* routine and a schedule; the white picket fence, kids, a dog, *a family*. I wanted to wake up, go to the gym, write, run my blog, start that garden, and see my friends.

I didn't want to travel the way I had been traveling anymore. I had seen the world from a backpack enough times.

Charlotte went to travel with her friends around Cairns, while I went to Perth to visit a friend. Away from her and with time to think, I realized I couldn't go to New Zealand. All I could think of was home, my bed, my roommates, and a stable life.

In Perth, I realized the truth: my travel burnout was permanent. It was time to put away the backpack.

I didn't want to travel anymore. I wanted the exact opposite of that. I knew in my heart this was the right thing to do—the same way I knew leaving all those years ago was the right thing.

I had grown over the last decade, and the last six months had given me the answer to the question Scott's death had brought up: what did I really want?

I wanted a home.

As I began to picture New Zealand, my panic attacks came back. The idea of sightseeing and working at once, never giving either the full attention it deserved and feeling guilty for that, was just too much for me. I was too unhappy on the road.

How would I break this to Charlotte?

What would I say? How would she take it?

When I looked at Charlotte, I could picture the life we'd start together. I could picture our home, minivan, kids, and garden. But I could never ask her to change her travels for me. I couldn't take that from her. I had spent ten years as a nomad. I knew how long she had been waiting to do this. I could never make her choose and, if I had made her, she would have resented me for it. This was *her* trip.

And I knew first hand how important they are.

When I met Charlotte again in Sydney, I broke the news to her: I couldn't go to New Zealand with her. It would break me. I was trying to break a cycle and, as much as I loved her, I needed to heal a bit and get my head in order. Going to New Zealand would only exacerbate the problem. She was coming back to the United States in three months, and there was no reason I couldn't be the one who greeted her at the airport. We could still talk every day.

She cried and said she understood.

Over the months, we stayed in touch, but our chats grew less frequent. A gulf of my own making had developed between us. She traveled all over the country and I laid the foundations of a routine. My passport collected dust in my drawer. I woke up early every day. I went to the gym again. I started cooking again. My eye twitch faded away. My anxiety became less severe. My panic attacks went away. I grew more peaceful. I never once missed travel.

But I did miss Charlotte. As I lay in bed at night in my apartment, I wondered what she was up to. What was she doing over in New Zealand? I had no idea, because she went longer and longer without updating me.

In my mind, I still held out hope that when she came back to the States we would pick up where we left off. Yes, we fought in Melbourne, but it wasn't over anything big.

By the time Charlotte came home, I had left New York for a quieter apartment in Austin. When she came to Austin to visit some friends, we agreed to meet up. We talked about the past few months, and our future. We opened up to one another, and it became clear that we had never really fully expressed our feelings and our thoughts. To her, when I got on that plane home, our relationship had ended. The conversations online and through chat never really made me sense the pain and hurt she was feeling.

To me, she had never really understood the extent of my panic attacks, anxiety, and desire to slow down. I had retreated into my shell and thought I had explained things well to her, but it turned out we both had walls up.

We both read each other wrong.

And now it was too late.

She was going back to New Zealand, and I was home where I wanted to be. There was no way to go back to where we were before. It would be like chasing ghosts. There was nothing left to say.

We got up and hugged, and then I watched her walk away.

It's strange seeing someone walk out of your life after envisioning a future with them—marriage, kids, old age. Like a writer getting a blast of inspiration, I saw how the story developed, played out, and even ended. But then an unexpected wind blows all the pages out the window and the story is gone forever.

Timing is everything. Charlotte and I started out with a future but soon found we were in different places in our life. That is life. You grow and change over the years and hope that the person walking beside you grows and changes with you. You hope your roads run parallel. You hope that you are running the same race.

For a while, it felt like we were. But before long it became clear that, while we were in the same race, we were at wildly different points. She had many laps to go, and I was at the finish line.

⊕

WHEN I STARTED OUT ON MY TRAVELS, *home* was a dirty word. It was a boring place where you commuted to work and sat in traffic and missed the train. It was where life grew stale. A place of death.

I didn't want to stay home. I wanted adventure. I wanted excitement. I didn't want to waste my days inside an office building, and the more I traveled, the less appealing home became to me. Coming home meant boredom. The road was where I felt alive, and I couldn't let go of that.

But now, having uncovered the reasons for my panic attacks and feeling drawn toward starting a home with someone I loved, I realized another deep truth: there is nothing wrong with change. Even Peter Pan grew up. Even I had to stop traveling.

I had just been too blind to see it before.

I had been wrapped up in my nomadic identity for so long that I failed to realize that the original reason I left—to become a better, more confident me—no longer applied, and hadn't for years. I had all that I needed in front of me. I had friends. I had work that I loved. I had stories. I could talk to strangers. I liked trying new things. I could make conversation.

But most, I was okay with myself. I was satisfied with who I was, what I liked, and everything I did.

Peaks and valleys, ebbs and flows aside, I had come home from my original trip the person I wanted to be.

That is what finding home feels like.

Originally, the reason I loved Thailand so much was that it was a place that had all the elements I thought a life should have. But home isn't a place. It's not a destination. It's not where your heart is. Home is wherever you are in the world. It didn't matter if I was in New York City, Austin, Bangkok, Paris, or my parents' house outside of Boston.

For me, after 2008, home was a million places, because home is where you feel at peace with yourself, and I was comfortable everywhere. That's something I learned as a nomad, and something I won't let go of even after I stop being one.

With Charlotte, I was holding onto the past because in the past, the travel version of me was the one who felt in control of his life. Why would I want to give that up? Travel had made me who I was, and I thought leaving it meant going back to the old me.

But it didn't. There is no old you. There is just the you that you are right now. You are always a work in progress. You are always ever changing. The world moves on, time passes, people come and go, and the future is always uncertain.

As they say, that is life.

But it took me a long time to come to realize that.

I had resisted change for so long because I wanted to resist the passage of time.

I wanted to be a young backpacker forever. I wanted to live in the nomadic bubble, the place where Charlotte and I found love, where life was carefree, everyday was Saturday, and it was always an adventure because I thought it was the only place I could be happy. It was where I found myself—and thought that was the only place I could be the me I wanted to be.

But I was wrong.

As I sat on my balcony overlooking Austin, I realized that I could make my life anything I wanted it to be. Being happy didn't depend on traveling—or on *not* traveling, for that matter. Being happy with who I'd become felt like something that was true no matter where I was.

Most travel memoirs are about escape—and they end in either death or defiance. People just keep pressing on; or they croak. My story isn't so canned and predictable. Spoiler alert: I'm not still a backpacker clutching to a dream, and I don't die at the end of this. This is a deeper, more elastic story than that. It's about what you find at the end of ten years of ceaseless, relentless travel.

What you find is that truism of self-discovery so well expressed by Jon Kabat-Zinn: *Wherever you go, there you are.*

What you find, after enough breakups, bad habits and head-splitting headaches in hostels with beautiful views, is what Emerson meant when he referred to travelers who travel away from themselves, "he carries ruins to ruins."

So you look deep into that part of yourself and decide to give regular, real life a chance again. In one place. For good. You think you've found the girl you want to settle down with and you start planning it out in your head. You get that same exciting feeling that you did when you first started traveling—that this is the right adventure for you. Of course, real life is never simple. The girl—she doesn't want to settle down. *She wants to travel.* But you move anyway, hoping that when she's ready, she'll come to you. You commit to it.

My friend Bill likes to say that trees grow because they have roots.

I, the acorn, had been blowing in the wind long enough. If I wanted to grow any further, I'd have to grow roots so I could continue to reach for the stars.

It took a few months in Austin for the restlessness to wear off, for me to find my bearings.

It was easier said than done. Even when I cut down on traveling to what I thought was "slowing down," my friends joked that I was still barely around!

That December, I did an interview with Andy Steves (son of the famous travel writer Rick Steves). Knowing I was cutting back on my traveling, he asked about going from nomad to non-nomad.

"Is it hard to settle down after such a long time on the road?"

"It's even harder than deciding to travel," I firmly replied.

But it's the hard journeys, you learn as a traveler, that are most worth the effort and the struggle and the risk.

⊕

TO ME, the road is and always will be a place of wonder and endless possibility. It's where magic happens. But you can find wonder and magic wherever you are. You just have to look closely enough. And sometimes you don't have to look very far at all. Sometimes, believe it or not, it's right outside your front door.

Most people think of travel as this thing you do in faraway

lands. They think that travel is about getting on flights to places where people don't speak your language, places with different customs, a different history, different food, and different climate. *That's* travel. It's the act of going to the exotic.

I don't agree with that definition of travel.

To me, travel is the act of going somewhere new, doing something new, meeting someone new, and connecting to as much of it that feels right and good to you.

That can be in a country half a world away. It can be in the next town over. Or it can be a staycation where you explore your own town (which I think is always a good thing).

Travel is the art of discovery. It's about visiting a place you haven't been before, and learning both about the things that make it unique and the things that tie it to the greater human experience. A place like that can absolutely be your own backyard. It's something that took me a decade of travel to fully appreciate but it's also something I've known since the very beginning of my travels.

When I started my inaugural trip around the world, in fact, I drove across the country for the first time. It was the summer of 2006 and I set out for a two-month road trip around America before I was to fly to Europe. I'd never been off the East Coast and wanted to see my backyard before I saw the world. How could one understand the world if one didn't understand his home?

The great American road trip in the model of Jack Kerouac or John Steinbeck seemed too irresistible to pass up. It was an opportunity to live the great American dream. I imagined open roads, interesting diner stops chatting to locals and waitresses, and exploring the great national parks of the West I'd always seen pictures of.

Having never left the comfort of my Boston-born bubble, I had some firm, preconceived notions about hillbilly Southerners, conservative cowboys, and middle-class rural America from ingesting a diet of cable news and pop culture throughout my life.

Though they were my countrymen, I couldn't think what we would agree on. I viewed them as gun-toting, backward, hate-filled, religious zealots who wouldn't match my youthful liberal outlook on life. I looked down on them with the vanity of youth.

Driving around the states shattered many of my preconceived notions. America is a diverse nation with significantly divergent political beliefs and cultural traditions from area to area, state to state, and city to city. From the slowness of the South, to the fast pace of the East Coast, to the cowboys of the West, and to the small towns of the Corn Belt, each region has its own unique fingerprint. But day to day, what I discovered is that we essentially live the same lives, share the same hopes, dreams, and stresses. Maya Angelou once said, "Perhaps travel cannot prevent bigotry, but by demonstrating that all peoples cry, laugh, eat, worry, and die, it can introduce the idea that if we try and understand each other, we may even become friends." Indeed, meeting new people in new towns who lived differently than my East Coast lifestyle, I learned that, in the famous words of *Le Monde*, we are all Americans. These people were not the stereotypes of my imagination.

And, when I went on another cross-country road trip in 2015, this time with the wisdom of age, I learned those things all over again.

The trips taught me that no matter how many microcultures and differences we have, our common core beliefs and positive outlook make me hopeful our future will be bright. It taught me to appreciate the undervalued concept of home travel.

Travel teaches us a lot about the world. It gives you an understanding of a place that you can only get from firsthand experience. When I hear people talk about a country or a city or a people negatively, I always ask, "Yeah, but have you been there? Have you talked to anyone from there?" As travelers, we know the truth in Maya's words. We know that travel can break down barriers. We know travel can foster understanding.

Yet we never bother to do in our own backyard what travel does for us out on the road. As I traveled the world, so many travelers told me that I'd seen more of their country than they had. I reminded them they could travel their country, too. They could do what I did. I'd ask them what was stopping them, but I already knew. It was that nagging belief that "home" is a boring place from which all adventure has fled.

When you open your heart to your home, you open your mind to the world. It gives you permission to wonder: What is this land where I'm from? What is this world I live in? Who are these other people that share it with me? How are they like me? How are we all like each other?

And travel, both home and abroad, will give you the answers.

OVER MY TEN YEARS OF TRAVEL, I became confident in my own skin, made some of my closest friends, figured out who I was, and learned what I wanted. I was a proud nomad. Now it was time to let that go and to move on with my life. The spirit of "Nomadic Matt" will always be with me, but my nomadic days ended when I waved good-bye to Charlotte.

If I learned anything from travel—from all the people and experiences—it's that life is too big to fit in any box. Travel helps you learn that quickly. It makes you grow faster than you thought possible, putting you in different, uncomfortable situations in foreign lands with different customs.

But it's a lie to say you can't take that growth home. That home has to be boring. That home has to be depressing.

The real world can be like travel, if you approach it with the spirit of openness, curiosity, and adventure.

I used to believe adventure was always outside the borders of "home."

But a place is only as boring as you are. Adventure and activity isn't something that just happens. It is something that must be sought out.

Whether in the next town, the next country, or the street a few blocks away, finding home—and finding yourself—is about going out and asking questions and seeking answers.

I was ten years a nomad.

Now I am someone rooted in place.

Someone who's embraced the realization that each day can bring an adventure.

No matter where you are in the world.

ACKNOWLEDGMENTS

A BOOK IS A GROUP EFFORT and I want to thank a lot of people!

First, I want to thank my agent, Byrd Leavell, for helping me shepherd this book from idea to publication. Thank you for believing in and helping me get this book brought into the world.

Second, I'd like to thank my editor, Daniela Rapp, for also believing in this book. Thank you for working with a practical, nuts-and-bolts travel writer as he took his first dip into the world of memoir and literature.

Third, I'd like to also thank Ryan Holiday and Nils Parker for being my Yodas during this process. As someone who had never been through this process before, thank you for providing wisdom and help from proposal to finish.

Acknowledgments

I'd like to thank Fey, Torre, and Jodi for providing early feedback on the structure and content of the book. Thank you for helping point me in the right direction.

Thank you to all the readers of my website who have made this crazy journey possible and have stuck with me through the years of constant mind changing. Sorry for the whiplash.

Thank you to my team—Erica, Raimee, Chris R, Chris O, Mike, and Candice—for helping me grow my website over the years and dealing with my constant scattered brain nature. Thanks for also keeping the ship afloat while I worked on the book!

Thank you to all the people who I met in my travels who have shaped my life. The memories we share have been some of the best of my life. Thank you for helping me find the true me.

Finally, thank you to my mom, dad, and sister for all the love and support over the years and dealing with my constant wanderlust when all they wanted was for me to stay home. Sorry for all the gray hairs.

APPENDIX

19 Lessons from a Decade of Travel

In this book, I've tried to share with you all of the lessons I learned from a decade on the road—a decade as a nomad. But, for your convenience, I've also collected them here. To give you some lessons and advice for when you embark on the road. For when you get burned out and need a little inspiration. I know how important it is to travel light, so you have my permission to rip these pages out of the book and take them with you on the road.

1. IT'S NOT THAT HARD.

Every day, people get up, go out the door to travel the world, and survive and thrive. Kids as young as eighteen years old make their way around the world without any problems. All that worrying and fear I had before my first trip was for naught. Once you hit the ground, getting around a place is the same everywhere. Trains, buses, taxis, tours. There's a universality to travel. This traveling thing was a lot easier than people make it out to be. And you're not the first person to do it. There is a well-worn trail that makes it easy for first-timers to find their way. If an eighteen-year-old can do it, so can you.

2. YOU LEARN A LOT OF LIFE SKILLS.
People who travel are better adjusted and less socially anxious. Traveling around the world has taught me how to be more social, be adept and more flexible, and, most importantly, understand nonverbal communication a lot better. It has made me more independent, more open, and, overall, just a better person. There's no reason to be scared that you might not have "it" in you. In truth, no one does. "It" is only learned by experience. You'd be surprised how often you'll surprise yourself.

3. YOU ARE NEVER ALONE.
It may seem scary just throwing yourself out there and talking to strangers, but we are all strangers in a strange land. At the end of the day, everyone is very friendly. It took me a while to get used to just saying "hello" to strangers, but now it seems like second nature. Your fellow travelers are just like you. They are alone in a strange place and are looking for others to be with. People travel to meet other people, and that means you. You'll find that when you travel alone, you'll never really be alone.

4. YOU MEET SOME OF YOUR CLOSEST FRIENDS TRAVELING.
Whether it was in a restaurant in Vietnam, on a boat in Thailand, or walking into a hostel in Prague, when I least expected (or wanted) to meet people was when I met my best friends—those with whom I'd have the longest-lasting and most fulfilling relationships. And even though you may not see them for years, you still end up at their weddings, Christmas dinners, or family celebrations. Tight bonds are forged in travel—distance and time can't break them.

5. RELATIONSHIPS COME AND GO ON THE ROAD.

The nature of travel doesn't always lend itself to long-term romantic relationships. It's hard to make something last when everyone moves in different directions and holidays end. If you get too attached too often, you'll have nothing but heartache. Relationships on the road can be special—if you agree to live in the moment and savor the time you've been given. Dwelling on the future will only keep you from making that leap.

6. BUT CHASE THE ONES YOU LIKE.

Once in a while, though, you'll find someone you really connect with. Meaningful romance on the road *does* happen. And when you have nowhere to be and no place to go other than where you want, sometimes there is no reason not to follow someone you care for. Don't force yourself to say another good-bye if you don't have to. Pursue it even if the distance seems too vast and the circumstances not right, because you never know where it could lead or how long it might last. Once in a while, you meet the one—so don't blow it.

7. IT'S GOOD TO TRY NEW THINGS.

I used to be a very rigid person, but traveling has helped me loosen up and expand my worldview. I've pushed myself to the limit, eaten new food, taken cooking classes, learned magic tricks and new languages, tried to conquer my fear of heights (unsuccessfully so far), and challenged my established views. Travel is all about breaking out of your comfort zone and enjoying all the world has to offer. You'll never know what you like or are capable of if you don't push your boundaries a bit.

8. BE ADVENTUROUS.

Doing the canyon swing was tough. So was jumping off the boat in the Galápagos. As was eating the maggots in Thailand and caterpillars in Africa. Then I got my butt kicked in Thai boxing. And while I won't do most of those ever again, I don't regret trying any of them. Scare yourself once in a while. It makes life less dull. See point #7.

9. THERE IS NO SUCH THING AS A MISTAKE.

No matter what happens on the road, it's never a mistake. As a wise person once said, "your choices are half chance, and so are everybody else's." When you go with the flow and let the road unfold ahead of you, there's no reason to have regrets or think you made a mistake. You make the best decisions you can with the information at the time. I may not have ever found romance with Heidi but I don't regret the choice I made. I did the best I could. And, in the end, learned that the journey is the adventure.

10. DON'T BE CHEAP.

When you travel on a budget and need to make your money last, it's easy to be cheap. But why live like a pauper at home to save for travel so you can skip the food in Italy, the wine in France, or a sushi meal in Japan? While it is good to be frugal, it's also important to splurge and not miss out on doing once-in-a-lifetime things. Who knows when you will get another chance to dive in Fiji or safari in Africa?! Take every opportunity. You won't regret it.

11. THAT BEING SAID, DON'T BE WASTEFUL.

But remember you aren't made of money, so don't always feel like you need to party with your new friends every night or do every activity in a new place. Sometimes it's okay just to sit around and relax or cook your own meal. Be frugal, but not cheap. Most of all, be conscious and deliberate about your money—decide what's worth spending on, and what's not.

12. DROP THE GUIDEBOOK.

I know guidebooks were an important part of my story (heck, I write them for a living), but the other important part was learning to get beyond them. Don't be so glued to a book. You can travel fine without it, especially with so many good alternatives on the internet these days. You'll buy it and hardly use it anyway. Just ask people for tips and information. That will be your best source of information, especially for those off-the-beaten track destinations and hole-in-the-wall restaurants that no one's ever heard of but serve the best food you can imagine.

13. IT'S NEVER TOO LATE TO CHANGE.

Even if you aren't the traveler or person you want to be in your head, it's never too late to change. Travel is all about change. The more you say "tomorrow," the less likely it is that tomorrow will ever come. Traveling has shown me aspects of my personality I wish I didn't have, and it's also shown me I'm really lazy. I've always lived by the phrase "carpe diem," but some days I don't "carpe" much of anything. Every day is a chance for a fresh start and a new you. Don't let your past define you.

14. RELAX.

Life is amazing. The universe unfolds as it should. Relax and just go with it. You can't change the future—it hasn't happened yet. Just make the best decisions you can today and enjoy the moment. Don't get caught up trying to see all the "must-sees." There's nothing wrong with spending a day playing games, reading a book, or lounging by the pool.

15. LEARN MORE LANGUAGES (SERIOUSLY).

There're some great benefits to not knowing the local language—like miming out "chicken" to let the lady know you want eggs for breakfast—but learning languages is very helpful when you travel, and works out great when you meet other travelers. There's also nothing like surprising people by speaking their language. Moreover, knowing basic phrases will endear you to locals, who will appreciate the fact you went the extra mile. You'll find people will be much more helpful, even if you struggle to say hello.

16. WEAR MORE SUNSCREEN.
Seriously. Science has proven it helps, and with all that beach time you may get on your travels, you could always use a little more. Being tan is great. Having skin cancer is not. SPF up.

17. PEOPLE ARE GOOD.
All over the world, I have encountered amazing people who have not only changed my life but have gone out of their way to help me. It's taught me that the old saying is true: you can always depend on the kindness of strangers. My friend Greg taught me long ago not to be guarded against strangers. That lesson changed everything for me. When you travel with an open heart, unexpected goodness will happen. 99.9999 percent of the people in the world aren't murders, rapists, or thieves. There's no reason to assume someone is trying to get over on you. Sometimes people are just trying to be friendly.

18. THERE'S NO SUCH THING AS MUST-SEE.
This is your trip. No one else's. Everyone's journey is their own. Do what you want, when you want, and for how long you want. Don't let anyone tell you that you aren't a real traveler for skipping the Louvre, avoiding some little town in Peru, or deciding to party in Thailand. This is your journey. You owe no one an explanation.

19. JUST GO.
Above all: find a way to travel as often as you can to all the destinations you dream about. They will change your life. I know they changed mine.